WEST
CUMBRIA
ON
THE EDGE

JOHN SCANLAN

In Certain Places
Preston, UK
www.incertainplaces.org

West Cumbria: On the Edge
First published by In Certain Places,
University of Central Lancashire, 2019
With the support of the Samuel Lindow Foundation

Photographs by the author, except those listed on p. 115.

ISBN: 978 0 99304 985 9

Book design by Bonnie Craig, www.bonnie-craig.com
Printed and bound by T. Snape & Co., Preston, Lancashire.

Contents

O C E

N V S

Chapple of the grune
Cardronok Whitridge
Kirkbyr
Fenwland Bainton pa
Thelaithe Wampull
Skinnoranesse
Langnewton
Edulthe Kirkyetes
Wisby east Holme Leson hall
Tho Lire Souterfeld Bloncongey
Old Manboro Brownfeld Wartog
Newton in Ardale Crockdale
Dubmill Absear's
Allonbye Mfotte Blemrose
Crosby Allureton Olterfide Watkynbor Bolton
Camonbye Floxmund Hodell
Garnesse Mentosbecon
Brayton Redmain Sunderland
Elisboro Tosantserd Isle
Wirggy Brickirke
Flimbre Camerton Dronouby Hothwater
Rikon Ed. Setmurthe
Seaton Brougton
Chsten Ed. Lawrton COKERMOTH
Dstinton Lamploy COCKERMOTH Comleton
Moresby Vflck
Arundon Bardsey hall
Cafauld how Brakenthwaite
Whthaven Enerdale Loutsfwater
Dent hill
COPE LAND
Dent hill Copeland forest
EGRENOND
Ifale
St Johns beckermond
St brides
Caudey Nether Wafdaleheno
Ponsonby
Sedfeld Gosfforthe
Seafcall hall
Drig Irton
Carleton Monaster
RAVENGLO
Wamburthwaite
Corno
Seaton
Bowtell
Whulloh
Whatyfhm

WIRKINTO

West warde forest

The Ward
The mynes
IERBYE Ancentre Clabok
Vdale Mofedale
Armythwaite
Bafinkhwate Shaddow hall
Crofthwaite
KESWICK
Thornthwate Portingskale Derwent
Lorton Brathwaite
Newlande
chap Watenlath
the grange Armuthst
Borrodale
Wosdale
chap
Blenj
Nether Wafdaleheno
Shyrefpot
Vprsoitesworth
Myrredale
E Ardale
Dalegarthe
Black-hall
Fourn
Southwate
St Tohos
Vffay p
Kirkb
Broughton

CHRISTOPHORVS SAXTON DESCRIPSIT

Scala Miliarum

AVGVSTINVS RYTHER ANGLVS
SCVLPSIT AN DÑI 1576

It is not down in any map; true places never are.

Herman Melville, *Moby Dick*

Workington One of the numerous locational markers that can be found on the land around the Port of Workington. These are intended as aids to vessels as they navigate the narrow channel into port during changing tidal conditions. For the non-seafaring visitor to this area – which is popular with local people – these markers have something of the quality of abstract sculptures that have been left dotted around the landscape.

Locations

West Cumbria: the North West of England, almost as far north and west as it was possible to go in England. There, on the overlooked edge of the Lake District, was a place that was both strange and unfamiliar to me. But it was here that I found myself, digging my way through the abstractions: graphics, virtual renderings, lots of maps. Road atlases, Ordnance Survey maps – from the 1800s, the early 1900s – fragments of geological maps found during interminable internet forays, very old maps that looked as if they were illustrated with allegorical figurines floating over the landscape and mythical giant fish breaking the surface of the water just off the coast, maps of Roman Britain, maps found in old tourist guide books, a tattered 1950s Mobil road map of Northern England, dynamic interactive maps conjured up on computers and smartphones that allowed me to pinch and zoom – seemingly getting closer and closer – and to watch as roads and place names suddenly surfaced. Like a child digging a hole in the garden in the hope of reaching Australia, I was beginning to think all this effort was going nowhere fast.

It was a plunge into strangeness, something I couldn't easily make sense of, certainly not at the beginning, nor for months afterwards. But lately – I had to keep reminding myself – I had become much more familiar with my surroundings. One question nonetheless continued to preoccupy me: what was this place? It was enough to send me out on the road, heightening my receptivity to the little details that various people whose paths I crossed would volunteer.

In some of those older maps, particularly those from the 17th and 18th centuries, I couldn't help but observe the proximity of Scotland in the spaces that cartographers of previous ages tended to leave blank just because they were not the places being represented. Sometimes the empty space would be marked with just enough information to identify an otherwise blanked out territory. 'Part of Scotland', one of them read, the words being all that occupied a blank space that was cut off as the squared-off map reached its edge. On one map, I noticed with interest a handful of place names that had some personal resonance, which were dotted around the blankness where the words 'Part of Scotland' might otherwise appear.

These impressions – broadly geographical, as I groped around for something more substantial – would soon become clearer as I absorbed a welter of other information that allowed me to see the same thing in a different light. I discovered a place as unique in character as any other place once it becomes the focus of attention. I seemed to have arrived at a place of exploding mines and collapsing streets, of red men in iron fields, of cottaged rows that stand like exposed dry-stone dykes in fields where the flatlands meet the more familiar Cumbrian hills, of intense coastal sunsets and creeping darkness moving over the plains on summer nights, of military science and weapons testing, of urban horses grazing in the most unlikely places – as if the surrounding townscapes were merely a stage set plonked down in the middle of fields – of old mine works that look like appendages to baronial homes, of Roman forts and ruins whose remains now lie beneath other, newer, buildings and farmland, of the fleeing Mary Stuart, Queen of Scots, concerned for the safety of her neck, of shipwrecks and sailors, sea bathers and salt panners, of coal and tobacco barons whose names live on in

Whitehaven Harbour The steep slope leads towards the harbour, obscured here, but with the remains of former mineworks – including the chimney stack known as the Candlestick – visible. The atmosphere today is much changed from that recounted by Paul Theroux in his 1982 book, *The Kingdom by the Sea*, when his walk along this route from St Bees Head to Whitehaven was accompanied by the 'smell of the coal and potash' before the town came into view.

street and place names everywhere, of Georgian towns in pastel colours and of 17th-century visitors searching out new, exotic experiences descending into the deepest mines in the world at Whitehaven. And, not least, perhaps, this was the place of the 'Atomic Men', who have, for more than half a century, nurtured – whether they are aware of it or not – a vision of what might be called the *technological sublime*, which is now inseparable from perceptions of this place. Their arrival was not just the source of a particular history, but also a sci-fi future that is as near infinite as human experience – whose rhythms of seasons, years and anniversaries maintain a connection between the present and the immediate future – can probably comprehend.

There is no way of evening out or redistributing the attributes of one part of Cumbria and the other. It is simply not a place with a singular, uniform character. It contains different worlds. But it is this sense of, at times extreme, contrast that affords an opportunity for a traveller to move from the 18th-century mountain sublime – found in the Lake District – to the 21st-century technological sublime in the space of a few miles. Both worlds are extreme in their own terms and character and extreme in their almost total difference from each other. And for those reasons Cumbria remains a place that is 'partly very well known and partly not known at all'.[1]

To encounter strangeness in an unfamiliar place is not unusual. In fact, it is probably the first and primary experience or sensation encountered at those times when we find ourselves in new surroundings. The effect that this has on what we see, hear and smell also shapes our impressions and in that respect produces a sense of heightened aesthetic awareness that is capable of

There is no way of evening out or redistributing the attributes of one part of Cumbria and the other. It is simply not a place with a singular, uniform character.

bringing the distinctive atmosphere of a place to our attention.[2] This is something that any tourist who has encountered a foreign culture will understand. But the atmosphere of a place is also subjective enough, or dependent on the senses to such an extent, that whatever it is that makes it up will be fleeting and changeable, and – of course – informed by mood and expectation, which is to say, something far removed from the more objective abstractions of things like maps, which produce another kind of picture of the same places. When the architectural historian John Martin Robinson visited Whitehaven in the mid-1980s, for instance, it was to look at the Georgian streets and buildings of England's first post-medieval town. But he was unable to avoid the stranger's impulse to go after the more intangible characteristics of the place that helped to provide some context for understanding its built historical character. While the maritime era that had made the town had all but vanished, its atmosphere nonetheless lingered on – a sort of ghostly emanation of a past – in the smell of salt and mud as he approached the harbour from the town and 'the clatter of nautical junk lying around on the quays, and the cries of seagulls'.[3]

In other words, for the insider in their familiar environment, it requires a special effort to foreground the qualities that the stranger encounters – to see beyond the functionality of a place within their daily existence and to pay much attention to intangible qualities such as 'atmosphere'.[4] To step out with a camera or a notebook, on the other hand, is one way of opening oneself up to the strangeness of the otherwise familiar place and being capable once again of seeing and feeling what is perhaps the most 'comprehensive property of any place', which – according to some – would be its *spirit*.[5]

What I found out about West Cumbria, and what seemed to be most characteristic about it, was its existence on the edge of things. And the edges are

Whitehaven Marina Located between quays that seem to
have been named for some poetic or exotic purpose – Sugar
Tongue, Lime Tongue – the scene today is a marked departure
from the activity that once characterised this place.

many and varied: the edge that faces the sea; the edge that separates historically disputed frontiers and porous borders from outsiders; the edge that distinguishes it as a place from what I came to think of as 'the other Cumbria' of the Lake District; the 'edgeness' that belongs to a place that is largely unknown or has been forgotten; and, finally, the existential edge of *time*, because West Cumbria – from its industrial past to its nuclear future – has always been on the edge of time.

Places are thick with time, history and experience, which is why imagination and sensation have a role to play in how we 'narrate' and reflexively begin to make sense of them. This subjective input is something that becomes as important to a sense of place as any of the landmarks, built structures or facts that are more immediately and objectively within our grasp.[6] And sensation and experience, of course, produce 'images' that enliven the mind and feed the imagination.[7] This, then, is a book of my impressions of a place; snapshots, if you like, exploring my sense of West Cumbria's being on the edge.

To step out with a camera or a notebook is one way of opening oneself up to the strangeness of the otherwise familiar place and being open to its spirit.

Burgh by Sands The memorial to Edward I, who died at this spot in 1307. Located several miles from Carlisle and close to the Cumbrian coast, Edward – so-called 'Hammer of the Scots' – was on his way to the coast to sail across the Solway to quell a Scottish uprising that was moving in his direction, apparently inspired by the rumour that he was already dead. This could be considered as the northernmost point of what has always seemed to be a militarised coastline.

Frontiers

B orders and other territorial markings can easily be
seen from the present to be somewhat arbitrarily
or even accidentally drawn on the land. This may
be especially true when the disputes of the past are
long forgotten or overcome. Yet the existence of such
boundaries also, in some strange way, reflects the
historical settlement of long-festering grievances and
violent disputes, and in that respect usually brings an
end to the most deadly of conflicts. Seen in this way, a
border represents an agreement to butt out of each other's
business or at least to attempt in some measure to be
more civil than those ancestors who turned borderlands –
and certainly the border between Scotland and England
– into a bloody, muddy and dangerous place, 'the scene
of plunder and bloodshed', ravaged for long periods by
'savage incursions of both kingdoms alternately'.[1]

The uncertainty that became attached to the
borderlands was something that seems to have
contributed to the murky and unknown early history of
the place now known as Cumbria, a part of England that
even as recently as the 17th century was regarded as one
of the 'dark corners of the land'.[2]

I once asked a friend, who had spent decades
studying the statistical evidence of border disputes the
world over, what his work revealed to him – what it all
boiled down to. I was simply after some underlying truth
about how these lines drawn on paper changed the reality
on the ground. He told me that he couldn't speculate

about that, but the fact that these warring borderland regions are found everywhere suggests that international relations could really just be thought of in terms of local border disputes exploded onto some larger canvas – onto the world map, perhaps – and thus into some larger significance.[3] These places where differences rise up are just the locations where the most intractable of human disputes, drawn into history on a map, have their origin.

Cumbria, of course, was a place whose territorial boundaries frequently changed and whose land territory – or parts of it, at least – shifted back and forth between the two warring nations. It was a place that became, for a long time, a kind of lawless ambiguity.[4] It was a land comprised of an indeterminate space that was nonetheless cut through by a real line on the ground in the form of Hadrian's Wall, a fairly visible reminder of the struggles that the all-conquering Roman Empire had itself faced here in northern Britain. And some centuries after these invaders had abandoned their wall and their forts, just south of the present-day borderline that separates Scotland and England, was the place where Edward I – so-called 'Hammer of the Scots' – drew his last breath in 1307. He was 68 years of age – an old man at a time when the life expectancy for men was about half his years, bedridden with dysentery and rendered invisible enough that the rumour was that he was already dead. After rising from his sickbed to drive his men to war in person, he headed out west from Carlisle, making for the Cumbrian coast to sail across the Solway Firth to Scotland.

The centuries old militarised coast was succeeded more recently by submarine bases, weapons testing ranges, munitions factories and radio communications stations.

But he never made it and 'was forced to stop at Burgh by Sands, an isolated settlement close to the Cumbrian coast', the 'windswept wilderness' where he spent his last night on Earth.[5] The field at Burgh by Sands in which he died, set in a patch of land that served as some kind of base for military forays in all directions at that time, is today marked with a modest memorial to the man described as a great and terrible king.[6]

Elsewhere, away from its northern borderlands, Cumbria remained susceptible to invasion from a coastline that faced the Irish Sea and connected it to the larger waters beyond, which carried Scandinavian and Irish colonists onto its territory between the 5th and 8th centuries, which is to say, the Early Middle Ages. The last military invasion was by an expedition of the American Continental Navy in April 1778 during the American War of Independence, led by a transplanted Scot and former Cumbrian seaman named John Paul Jones, who brought his men ashore at Whitehaven with the intention of burning every ship in the harbour.

The ship he commanded, the *Ranger*, had been sent on its mission – the only American military force to come close to Britain – by Benjamin Franklin with instructions to 'harass shipping around the British Isles and, if possible, kidnap a well-known personage who could be exchanged for American prisoners held in England'.[7] As it turned out, Jones only set upon Whitehaven after being thwarted in a first attempt to kidnap the Earl of Selkirk at St Mary's Isle on the Solway coast. Sailing around the Irish Sea under a British flag and in search of a consolation prize or some action that might appease his restless men, he set upon the port that he knew very well and where he had begun as a cabin boy at 13 years old and ended up as chief mate on a Jamaican slave ship before finally joining the new Continental Navy when the American War of Independence broke out in 1775.

The attack on Whitehaven, however, failed – only one ship was destroyed – after some of the 30 or so men he took with him had broken into a tavern and ended up drunk on ale and whiskey. The expedition then headed back across the Solway Firth to capture the Earl of Selkirk, but failed in this venture too, departing only with the family silver as a prize in place of the absent nobleman.

It was an outcome that led this hero of the American War of Independence and 'father of the American Navy' to be seen as no more than a pirate in the country of his birth.[8]

More than a thousand years before, stretching from the north where Hadrian's Wall reaches its end at the Solway Firth to the south at Ravenglass, there had been a line of small Roman military settlements, with forts strategically located along the coastline to thwart invasion from the sea. This militarised coast was succeeded in the recent past by a more modern military presence at various points along the length of the modern Cumbrian coast: air force and submarine bases, weapons testing ranges, munitions factories and radio communications stations.

Today, on the promenade at Seascale, the hapless tourist – perhaps innocently enjoying an ice cream cone – will be made aware of the military presence as they proceed towards the beach. There, signs warning of nearby weapons testing and the possibility that live ordnance might reach the shore is probably enough to put off even the most ardent windsurfer or paddler – despite the contemporary rage for extreme sports. Unwitting pleasure boat users sailing in the direction of the marina at Whitehaven, who have not noted the 'danger area' marked on maps of the coastal waters, might be surprised to find heavy weapons going off in the near distance and wonder if they have sailed into some kind of war zone. Well, history would seem to answer in the affirmative.

•

It seems odd that this place – with a far from uneventful past – exists in the shadow of the calm that is the Lake District National Park, the Cumbria that most outsiders will know. It is, in so many ways, the opposite of that image of the natural idyll. For here in West Cumbria is a world that has rarely seemed to approach calmness, which kept on turning and starting over anew, a fact that seems entirely fitting for a place that stood on top of a land that was once rich in the energy source that powered the industrial revolution onwards: coal.

⌃ ***John Paul Jones*** Born and raised as Paul Jones on the Scottish side of the Solway Firth, Jones wound up establishing close ties with the American colonies at the time of the Revolutionary War. At the outbreak of hostilities between Britain and the American colonies in 1775, he joined the Continental Navy (as it was then known), becoming a hero of the revolution. He is remembered – on this Washington, DC monument – as the father of the American Navy.

Maryport West Cumbria can be seen as a kind of dispersed and micro urban region made up of a number of smaller urban settlements, which exist together as West Cumbria. It has a coastal boundary that was the same as the historic county of Cumberland (which is to say, it does not include the Furness peninsula, which was incorporated into

Prospects

The coastline of Cumbria is about 100 miles long, stretching from somewhere around the location of the picturesque northern hamlet of Rockcliffe – nestled in the armpit of the Solway Firth, right where Scotland and England meet – to Grange-over-Sands in the south.[1] '*West* Cumbria', though, has more often than not referred to a sub-region that was defined as much by its economy and industry as its geographical boundaries. Today it would be taken to refer to a smaller area – the former industrial West Cumberland – extending inland from the coast on the flatter plains that are wrapped around the mountainous terrain and natural boundary of the Lake District and from Silloth in the north (also a product of industrial Cumbria) to Seascale midway down the coast.

West Cumberland also included the town of Millom even further south, which is now – and always was – a place that seemed to exist in isolation, 'surrounded on three sides by the sea and with the exit to the north almost blocked' by the imposing form of Black Combe, a peak of 1970 feet, making Millom almost 'an island'.[2] It is a land that was once rich in minerals, with coal and iron ore (of the highest quality hematite found in the British Isles) driving the development of industry between the 17th and 20th centuries and the growth of towns like Workington, Whitehaven, Maryport, Cleator Moor and Egremont.

Such was the lure of its coastal location for industry that once, at the turn of the 20th century, the entire population of Dronfield, Yorkshire, moved to Workington, along with the relocating Cammell Laird steelworks that employed them, which itself was transported piece by piece to the Cumbrian coast to be reassembled.[3] What these transplanted men and women, and others drawn in from the countryside or more distant regions, would have seen and heard as they approached the steelworks daily was a very familiar sight in Sheffield – that of the glowing smelting ovens, sparks flying and giant towers pumping smoke and steam into the sky above, accompanied by the deafening sound of machinery and steam hammers. An isolated corner of England turned into a 24-hour-a-day world. Even today, when much of that industrial West Cumbria has vanished, there are still places where industry and production shape the environment, with the skyline around the coast on the approach to Workington still dominated by sights that are characteristically in tune with its past.

As a consequence of a shared history shaped by maritime, coal and steel industries, West Cumbrian towns have a common history and cultural heritage, but at the same time they retain their own distinctive characteristics.

Workington retains an air of grunginess in places and further out beyond the town is home to a fascinatingly 'subnatural' landscape – of mud, dankness and concrete rubble – where the land meets the sea around its port.[4] This is not a place whose character is beholden to idealised representations. It seems wholly fitting then that one of the best spots to get a sense of West Cumbria's compact coastal heartland is to be found at the top of a former slag heap located right on the land's edge.

The ground of this artificial hill seems precariously positioned and about ready to crumble into the sea itself, which is due in large part to the presence of a working quarry gaping on the other side of a flimsy wire fence and just a careless stumble below. To stand there beside an improvised memorial that is composed of a figure of Christ on the cross, looking out to the sea, is to stand on the remains of the industries that made this place. Now grassed over, the summit of this waste mound presents one of the best prospects from which the one-time industrial kingdom that stretched along the land's edge from Maryport to Whitehaven can be taken in, and the mountainous outline of the Lake District to the east can be seen rising up in the distance. To some locals, this small peak is known as 'How Michael' (to others, 'Slag Bank'). On some older maps it is also identified as 'St Michael's Mount' and is situated on what was once believed to be – much further back in time – the place where a Roman coastal signal station stood, one of many placed along this coastline.

Writing of this place in 1928, the renowned Oxford philosopher R. G. Collingwood, whose hobby was the history of Cumbria, described a summit – a modest 129 feet high – that was topped by a medieval pele tower, now also long gone.[5] But whatever it was in the past, the name 'How Michael' has stuck to this shifting and changing place. In the mid-19th century, there still existed a much older structure that one source described in 1860 as consisting of 'an ancient roofless building, generally known as the Old Chapel', which had also been called How Michael by those who worked the sea along this coast, and for whom it signalled a place of safety and shelter.[6] Its remnants, perhaps along with Collingwood's vanished pele tower, might well be mixed in with the industrial waste materials underneath the grassy mound that eventually rose up here.[7] To stand here is to stand on the verge of a history; one that is more subliminal than it is physically manifest.

The settlements that cropped up around the edge of this coastline were made up of people who had either moved west from areas inland or arrived by sea from places in Ireland, the Isle of Man and Cornwall and had earlier landed on the west coast after sailing great distances from Scandinavia and other places around the northern fringes of the British Isles. But the direction of travel since the second half of the 20th century has often seemed to be away from West Cumbria. Taken in its historical context, it is a development that is perhaps not so unusual. The mining communities that turned the west of Britain – from central Scotland to Cornwall – into hubs of industry and commerce seemed to have had the character of improvised and temporary places that might be swept aside like some stage set once their reason for being there was no more. Industrial places, almost anywhere one looked throughout modern history had been 'in large measure made up of incomers who remained itinerant and transient, moving (or being moved) to where the work moved'.[8] The condition of modern life that shaped such impermanence, especially when contrasted with the ties that communities had earlier had to the land, was one of existential homelessness. In practical terms, of course, this had implications – for the millions swallowed up by industry it meant living on the brink of unknown and uncertain futures and being at home not so much in any given place as in the readiness to move on when the time arrived.

If such rootlessness seems to belong to an earlier time in the development of industrial societies, it is also true to say that it was something that remained a reality in West Cumbria right into the 1960s as de-industrialisation spread here, as it did across entire regions of the western world, to devastating effect. One remedy prescribed by economists and other government advisors at the time, probably unable to see a future beyond the monolithic one-town industries that were dying, was 'emigration' – the logic being that towns whose industry had gone had no more reason to exist.

But this was something that often proved difficult to encourage in what the newspapers in the mid-20th century were frequently describing as the 'dying towns' of West Cumbria. Against the odds, perhaps, those who were suddenly seen as surplus to industrial requirements had put down roots.[9] Even in the depths of the worst 20th-century recession, in the 1930s, experts were baffled by accounts of unemployed Cumbrian men who had been found work in towns as far away as Kent, only to give up their new lives and walk all the way back home to hollowed-out towns like Cleator Moor.[10]

The fact that people were seen to be as disposable as the industries they served, of course, was and remains a global historical phenomenon. But in the case of West Cumbria it also reveals much about how the places they lived and worked, nestling amidst landscapes scarred from hundreds of years of exploitation, were seen almost as temporary abodes with no right of permanent occupancy.

⩔ *How Michael* On top of the artificial hill – a former slag heap – known as 'How Michael'.

Allonby 1981 One of a series of photographs taken by Raymond Moore, which manage to capture a sense of a place on the point of disappearance. This image was taken in Allonby at a time when the traditional industries that had shaped West Cumbria were gradually disappearing.

Images

If the edge of place can be thought of in terms of the undeniable sensation of reaching a boundary – evident in the smell and sound of the sea, for instance – there is nonetheless a more mysterious sensation of having reached some kind of limit that invites another way of looking. This sense of being on the edge of something – the edge of time or history and certainly at the point where the past and present seem to have split from each other, between one world and another – drew the attention of the photographer Raymond Moore in the 1970s and 1980s.

Moore, then regarded as one of Britain's foremost photographers, found himself pulled towards places in West Cumbria that seemed to have been overcome by a profound sense of marginality. He was particularly attracted to a number of seemingly unremarkable places along the Cumbrian coast, such as Allonby, Harrington and Silloth, which in his work take on a significance that exploded them out of their geographical position to make them more revealing of something much broader about the human condition in a changing world. To be there, he felt, was like being at 'the edges of civilization'.[1] Moore's images of West Cumbria provide glimpses into a place where things, in one way or another, look as if they have always been running out – at the edge of land, time and opportunity – or seemed to have already reached some kind of terminal, post-future condition.

Looking at the places that Moore took an interest in is a bit like finding snapshots from some imagined post-apocalyptic future. For some, the images 'look desperate and haunted', as if Moore 'had been chased across England to water's edge and was now dodging washing lines and garbage bins looking for a place to hold out'.[2] Even in the examples of his work that are devoid of human figures, and sometimes marked only with fleeting signs of life (a child's swing, a bedsheet catching the wind on a laundry line, a road sign poking out of a misty emptiness, animals looking as if they have been abandoned), he was able to articulate something of the cultural landscape that West Cumbria had become, almost as if he had grasped the 'cultural wholeness' of the place in its post-industrial moment, which these images, as fragments of something bigger, managed to convey.[3]

Today, as you drive between these small and somewhat unknown places, it is not unusual to catch glimpses of the occasional road sign pointing to the remains of Roman milefortlets dotted along the coast at regular intervals, which once marked the furthest edges of that empire. Moore, however, was not interested in Roman remains; he saw something else here, 'an unencumbered place', in the words of Melvyn Bragg; a place released from the burden of its traumatic history as the industrial civilisation that once ruled began to disappear from view.[4] For Moore, West Cumbria wasn't just a subject for his attempts to capture the atmosphere of 'loss' or 'aftermath' that seems to have pervaded his photography more generally, but it also became a place that he ended up having to live in, so compelling was its sense of being on the edge of things.[5]

> This was a place that suggested, in elusive moments, the possibility of catching more of that characteristic sense of edgeness, which, like light and shade, would 'flit across the face of things' and be gone.

Perhaps the lure of West Cumbria was also to do with the other (and more objective) atmospheric conditions of being in a westerly location by the sea – the nature of the light as it moved across the low-lying land on autumn days or the out-of-season ambience of holiday resorts that belonged to another era – that allowed people to make only the most 'marginal encroachments' into his field of vision.[6] But to Moore's eye, which sought out the grey and monochromatic in the way that objects stood against the light, this was a place that suggested, in elusive moments, the possibility of catching more of that characteristic sense of *edgeness*, which, like light and shade, would 'flit across the face of things' and be gone.[7]

The world that had disappeared to leave the seemingly vacant landscapes that Moore photographed is illustrated in another kind of image. In a postcard that is dated 1907, we can see a glimpse of West Cumbria in the days when it exported steel to the world. The view of Workington's Cammell Laird works that it shows – now long gone – presents an image that the recipient of the postcard (perhaps located in places far from Workington or Cumbria) might have regarded with wonder or horror, if not a mixture of both. Rising out of darkness, what we see is a remarkable image of the new industrial landscape that steel production ushered in, which functions in a much more general sense as a reminder that 'the space and time' peculiar to photography 'is none other than the world of magic.'[8]

It is true that ironworks had existed in this part of the county in the 18th century – in places like Seaton and Little Clifton – and in their time would have struck an impressive sight in the landscape, suitable enough to attract the attention of artists (such as George Robertson, who painted scenes of iron production in late 18th-century Wales) who sought out visions of a new industrial sublime. But even that was a world away from what we see here in this postcard, a scene that

has to be understood as the culmination of processes
that revolutionised industry later, in the 19th century.[9]
Even the best furnaces in the 18th century, prior to
the development of the new processes associated with
names like Henry Bessemer (whose surname can still
be seen around Workington today), could only function
intermittently. Modern steel production of the kind
seen in this image, as Fernand Braudel notes, actually
'divides two civilizations' – one before and the other
after modern steel production – and marks the older
world of production out as if it belonged to 'another
planet.'[10]

⌄ **Workington, 1907** A postcard view of the Cammell Laird steel
works when it dominated the skyline of Workington.

"Night Photography"
Cammel Laird & Co's Works, Workington

Copyright J.

> **What was produced here was steel that was shaped into the form of railway tracks that would leave this place to become wrapped around the world, binding together, caressing and connecting it.**

Even devoid of colour, one can imagine what's not there in this postcard: the drama of the changing colour of the sky, opened up like a vault by the light seeping up from the white-hot furnaces, across which floated the great plumes of thick smoke belching into the night. But there is nonetheless so much in an image like this that can only be suggested: the smell of the smoke and liquid metal, the clanging and screeching and deafening throb of metal presses as the products of this industry are stamped out. What was produced here was steel that was shaped into the form of railway tracks that would leave this place and gradually wrap themselves around the world, binding together, caressing and connecting its other places.

This was still a time when photographers and postcard makers – taking advantage of the novelty of the medium – liked to produce images of faked natural wonders (a man with a fishing rod landing a gigantic fish, oversized vegetables taking up whole wagons, ghostly apparitions) as they sought ways to sell images to a public curious to see things that were extraordinary in their dimensions or character, or in some way alluring and likely to draw visitors to unknown places.[11]

It is not too hard to imagine that the sheer spectacle of these steel works – the amazing light show that the work that went on during the nights produced – might have been one of the most impressive sights that a photographer who worked at night could turn his view towards. This was a kind of human-made industrial wonder that just kept on pumping out steel around the clock while the world around slipped into darkness and sleep. The darkness, in fact, lends it a rather different and more awe-inspiring quality than would have presented itself in the daytime. This image, as photographs often do, 'froze the time that passed by the camera into a two-dimensional still' to simulate or reproduce the existing world in its time, thus creating it anew for posterity each time a viewer sees the night wonder that it reveals.[12]

While photography, by the time this image was taken, was more than half a century old, it was only in the last decade of the 19th century that new processes emerged to solve the problem of working at night in weak, artificial light. This allowed night photography to develop as something close to an art form.[13] In Paris and New York, the photographers Brassaï and Alfred Stieglitz would win reputations as innovators by shooting the city at night, revealing it for the first time as an illuminated place that never stopped. Brassaï, driven to 'capture what so quickly escapes the eye and the memory', photographed night as it revealed itself in moonlight or under gas street lighting and in wet conditions that made the most unremarkable of urban characteristics – such as the rain-covered cobbled streets – suddenly luminous night wonders. Night photography, in other words, was a means of making the unremarkable look extraordinary.[14]

The darkness lends the image a different and more awe-inspiring quality than would have presented itself in the daytime. It froze time and captured a fragment of the existing world for posterity.

Postcards as postcards, however, are not art. Their function as a form of written communication – remaking 'pictures as writing surfaces' – makes them interesting, because it turns the medium into something that is capable of transporting the image into a literary and imaginative realm, where the sender can draw some kind of inspiration from what is depicted – perhaps something of the sense of time and place that one person wants to convey to another – and which might ultimately reach beyond the intentions of the photographer who produced the picture in the first place.[15]

Compared to today's digital snapshots taken on highly personal camera devices like smartphones, postcards stand out as simple, mass-produced images. At first glance, it makes them seem less personal. Yet the addition, in writing, of direct references to events, people, times and places may make them more evocative than the digital photographs that we are now able to take so easily and without much thought.

For anyone who has ever sought out particular images to encapsulate something of the character of a place, it is surely easy to see how this kind of image, with its drama of the power of invisible forces and actors, could make an impression on the recipient. Alongside the work of Moore, it provides a kind of counterweight to the more abstract composition of empty and abandoned space. The Cammell Laird works, like some small city that came to life set against the contours of the Lake District while the world around it slept, must have provided one of the most indelible sights of the sheer power of industry rising out of a landscape that could have been seen anywhere at the turn of the 20th century. Even with the backdrop absent in the dark, this postcard might have been a sharp reminder that this Cumbria was quite unlike that other place where rather different and *natural* wonders – lakes, hills, mountains – captivated the imagination.

As it is, the message written on the back of this 1907 postcard, sent on October 7th of that year, reveals that, in this case, it was simply a short message sent from one person to an absent friend – a Miss Turner, then attending the Home and Colonial College in Wood Green, London – with a brief summary of news from home and the simple hope that the image, no doubt reflecting the autumn nights in Workington, might remind her of 'this smoky place'.

Heading west In myth and history, the west was an idea and image of some final resting place where life's trials could be put aside. The power of the idea rests on the effect that the sight of the sun dipping below the horizon had on people. There, if only it could be reached – it was thought – paradise would be found.

Westwards

Cumbria is not only of the north, it is beyond 'The North', which is to say, a distance further on from that supposedly grim, cold and (the further north one goes) sparsely populated territory that has, for centuries, loomed in the English imagination. It is certainly true to say that if the parts of Cumbria that belong to the Lake District National Park supply your image of this place, then yes, it very much seems to possess the qualities of northerness. But, even then, it is not really that far north – people live further north in Scotland, in Shetland and beyond. And what's more important, certainly for understanding how misleading common perceptions can be, is that beyond the Cumbria that is known is a place whose character and identity has been determined far more by its western location than the fact that it lies north of most of the country.

If there are varieties of north, then it is no less the case that there are varieties of west. Interestingly enough, the revised and updated version of the 'Pevsner Guide' to Cumbria – containing new material from Matthew Hyde that fleshes out and adds detail to the often brief insights of the original text – described Millom not only as a town on the west coast of Cumbria, but also as a place that had the air of 'a Wild West town', meaning, presumably, the Wild West of Hollywood movies. The Market Square of 'grand facades' that seem to have 'nothing much behind them' struck Hyde as being reminiscent of the backless facades of a film set.[1] That perhaps says something about how hollowed-out Millom had become after its steelworks vanished, but it no less points towards its position on the edge of a frontier.

Further up the coast, the A595 road from Carlisle out to the west runs over an old Roman road that once connected the garrison in Carlisle to its western Cumbrian outposts – places like Maryport and Ravenglass that now form part of the 'Frontiers of the Roman Empire' World Heritage landscape. There, in the middle of farmland and approaching a small settlement called Red Dial, you may see a sign that reads, simply, 'Westward'. For a time, I was entertained by thoughts that this name could have been the result of some weary Roman commander or medieval pilgrim naming this spot on the land as a campsite on the road, within sight of the sun going down over the sea in the distance; one last place to stop before embarking on the last leg of the journey. Sadly, it turns out that the name was simply derived from the fact that the place was once the western ward of a medieval administrative unit of land called Inglewood – a local hunting ground – that came to be called Westward.[2] If your imagination allows, though, its mythopoeic resonance may enliven a contemporary journey west, over land where Romans once trudged.

The sense of a Cumbria that primarily existed on the western margins, or even as a *west-facing* society, was, in so many ways, later overwritten and concealed by the more powerfully resonating image of 'Lakeland', this inland mountainous place, which began to take hold in the mid-to-late 18th century. This was followed some 200 years later by the merging of Cumberland and Westmorland with other parts of Northumberland and Lancashire to make the new administrative county of Cumbria, in 1974, stretching the Cumberland that had once been described as a 'maritime county' into a new, imaginative construction.[3] An example of the power

of the 'Lakeland' or Lake District image is seen in the
perception of West Cumbria's best known writer, the poet
Norman Nicholson.

Nicholson's work, of course, was often concerned
with the Lake District, but that tends to obscure the
fact that he devoted as much of his life to 'documenting
the practice of everyday life' in Millom, the industrial
coastal town where he was born and where he lived all
his life.[4] It was a place, in his own words, where the 'tug
of the tide' drew his attention westwards and could set
the blood coursing through his veins.[5] The sea to the west
– the Irish Sea – is, of course, a channel of the northern
Atlantic Ocean, and it is the sense of being on the
edge of the Atlantic that perhaps informed Nicholson's

⌄   *Twilight* Under the evening sky on the beach at St Bees.

perceptions as they emerge in lines of verse that throw up an image of ships falling 'beyond the horizon where the sunset dips' as if, indeed, they were at the furthest western edge, disappearing with the sun into that mythic west beyond our sight.[6] If it is true to say that Nicholson was more interested in this sense of being on 'the dying Atlantic's edge' than he was in either the Lake District or the oceans and lands – the Americas – beyond the edge of the horizon and beyond what he saw, then it is no less true to acknowledge that the fact that Millom occupying this particular location supplied him with a sense of exposure to western atmospherics.[7] The exposed nature of Millom's coastal position meant that the associated climactic conditions were felt in ways that were not only palpable, but also impossible to ignore, even when it was possible to look out from the sheltered domestic space of the home. 'It is the Gulf Stream, that rains down the chimney, making the soot spit', Nicholson wrote. 'It is the Trade Wind that blows in the draught under the bedroom door'.[8]

The sense of a Cumbria that primarily existed on the western margins, or even as a west-facing society, was, in so many ways, later overwritten and concealed by the more powerfully resonating image of 'Lakeland'.

If there was any doubt that Nicholson was intimately obsessed with what lay to the west, then perhaps the epitaph on his headstone – somewhat belying the image of him as a 'Lakes poet' – reveals the truth of the matter. 'Sea to the West' presents the poet gazing out towards the western horizon as the day shifts into evening, his sight consumed by incandescent light 'exploding on the shore' and obscuring the lines and edges that mark out objects as distinct forms, as if he was being pulled into the mythical west, land where the sun hides.[9] The sensation of blinding light, his image of this light, provides a fitting epitaph for one whose days were spent looking out of a window towards the shifting, transforming horizon at the edge of his perceptual awareness:

Let my eyes at the last be blinded
Not by the dark
But by the dazzle.[10]

In terms of its atmospheric phenomena and conditions, West Cumbria may have more in common with western coastal areas elsewhere than it does with the wet, mountainous landscape nearby that it shares a name with. It is true that its rough pebble beaches, by the shores of the cold Atlantic, could never have spawned the kind of culture or lifestyle you find in the Pacific West – there's neither the climate nor the sandy beaches to conjure the ambience associated with that kind of coastal living – but it is undeniably a place that the interior landscape of Cumbria pushes out to the edge. It may seem odd to find oneself in what is usually perceived to be the north yet to be continually confronted by signs and allusions to something other than the grim and dank landscapes associated with northerness. The sight of pubs and restaurants with references to the 'Sun', for instance – there are numerous 'Sun Inns' around – seem to indicate that the names have more to do with the spectacle of the setting sun as a western phenomenon than with sun-soaked beaches.

The founding origin myth and power of the idea of *the west* – perhaps it sustained the Romans as they moved across this place – was as humanity's last destination, the Promised Land.[11] That was an idea that derived its power from the awe and wonder that the sight of the sun dipping below the horizon inspired, an inspiration for countless artists, including J.M.W. Turner – that great painter of sunsets, who found some sort of 'spiritual home' by the Solway Firth where Scotland and Cumbria fell within a single view. That sense of the west also supplied an archetype of heroic questing as portrayed by Virgil in the *Aeneid*, whose homeless refugee progresses westwards in search of the place where he might at last rest.[12]

Braystones Beach An aerial view of the strip of foreshore at Braystones, where holiday homes were first put up in the early 20th century. Similar houses appeared on another narrow strip at Nethertown. These have since become established as a settlement of permanent homes. On the immediate land side of the homes is the West Cumbria railway line, which further along at Parton runs through what train drivers know as Avalanche Alley, caught right between the sea and the fragile terrain that marks the edge of the land.

Shorelines

On the very margins of coastal places, as you move closer to the seashore, it is possible to see how precarious the human occupation of the land can be at such territorial extremes, particularly where life sprouts up in places that look as if they really belong to – or could be claimed by – the sea. The foreshore at the exposed edge of the sea is a space that changes character due to the movement of elemental forces that have remained beyond human control. This is the kind of place that provides the best vantage point from which the rhythms of the changing tidal conditions can be seen, subject to the celestial pull of gravity.

In the culture of maritime societies, unsurprisingly, the waters just beyond the comfort and safety of the land could quickly become transformed into an unknowable and forbidding place, where the most sober imagination conjoined with the spectacle of powerful atmospheric conditions could easily conjure up unwelcome or frightening visions – of ghosts and apparitions that lingered over shipwrecks or submerged vessels.[1] The sea has always been a violent and deadly place – an inhospitable, inhuman foe that indiscriminately gobbled up human lives – and, as such, an endless source for tales of death and destruction. In John Stagg's 1810 book of Cumbrian legends, *Minstrel of the North*, a traditional Cumberland verse titled 'Messenger of Death' retells the fate of a local nobleman lost at sea, whose spirit was said to haunt the shore near present day Workington:

Near where the foaming Derwent rolls,
its currents westward to the sea
There on the beach, by Solway's side
Lord Walter anxious waits for thee.[2]

More recently, further down the coast at St Bees, a
shipwreck from the turn of the 20th century, the masts
of which for many years would become visible as the tide
went out, provided a reminder of the deadly foe that these
settlements positioned themselves against. Images of
other ships run aground on the Cumbrian shore were also
produced as postcards, unusual mementoes of the power
of nature along the often-precarious shore.

Such exposure to nature's elemental power may
have been one reason why some of the earliest places
that existed along the Cumbrian coast and noted in the
historical record were monastic retreats. The most well-
known of these were at St Bees and Holme Cultram
(near present-day Wigton), perhaps because to realise
the monastic ideal in the Middle Ages it was necessary
to locate oneself in a remote and preferably dangerous
wilderness.[3] The choice of location would have been in
keeping with the practice of most of the monotheistic
religions, which had always valued wild or uninhabited
places, precisely because the absence of human comforts
was believed to be the best way of elevating the spirit
above its earthly material needs. It was one means whereby
the committed believer could be plunged into a condition
that arose out of the fact that a physical boundary – the
edge of the land, in this case – magnified the sense of
'living between two worlds'.[4] Following the example of the
desert fathers who founded these religions, whose tales of
days and nights roaming deserts may be familiar to us, the
holy men of north western Europe, lacking deserts, sought
out instead 'landscapes and environments which were
correspondingly forbidding' in their own way.[5]

Some areas along the coast of West Cumbria are
more marginal than others, not only in a spatial or

geographical sense, but also in terms of almost existing beyond the boundaries or zones of control that have, for centuries, established the very limit and geographic extent of places, as well as the ownership and legal status of the land. In such in-between zones you will find the perhaps not-so-visible line that separates the safe place from danger – from the violence of the sea.

Further north at Skinburness, a mile or so beyond Silloth and once a settlement in the possession of a nearby abbey at Holme Cultram, a neat row of bungalows today overlooks a picturesque coastal watch tower. But in the past, things were not so tranquil for those so precariously positioned by the sea. Nikolaus Pevsner lamented the fact that the Solway Firth had gobbled up the churches and other architectural gems of old Skinburness – indeed, the sea swallowed what was, up to the 13th century, an entire town – robbing posterity of the possibly significant structures here at what had been an important supply point for the armies of Edward I as the Wars of Scottish Independence raged in the borderlands.[6]

The remarkable (and apparently ad-hoc) ribbon development of dwellings found south of St Bees Head – stretched along precarious plots of land that find some shelter on the land side just beneath the route of the adjacent coastal railway line at Braystones, Nethertown and Coulderton – originally consisted of holiday homes: chalets for seasonal visitors from other parts of West Cumbria and further afield. They were planted on a space between the historic low and high water tidal marks, which marked the territory out as common land. As such, they existed beyond the reach of local government efforts to prevent anyone who fancied the impressive sea views from improvising their own beach home using old railway carriages or any other self-assembly options that might have been viable.[7]

> The sea has always been a violent and deadly place – an inhospitable, inhuman foe that indiscriminately gobbled up human lives – and, as such, an endless source for tales of death and destruction.

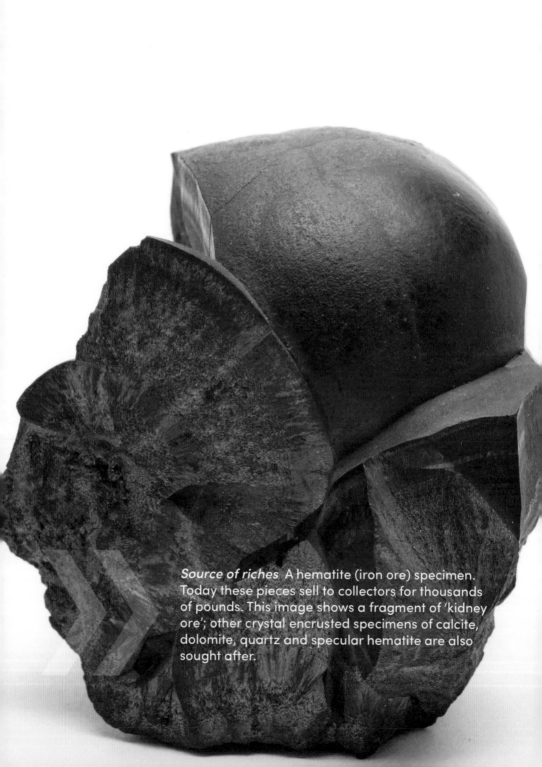

Source of riches A hematite (iron ore) specimen. Today these pieces sell to collectors for thousands of pounds. This image shows a fragment of 'kidney ore'; other crystal encrusted specimens of calcite, dolomite, quartz and specular hematite are also sought after.

Redlands

Several miles from the coast on land that reaches towards the edge of the Cumbrian mountains is the town of Cleator Moor. Along with a cluster of smaller neighbouring villages – Frizington, Moor Row, Bigrigg amongst them – it rose up in the mid-19th century to accommodate the incomers who by then were arriving in large numbers to work in the many mines that would eventually spread across this landscape, where the high-grade iron ore that had been discovered by local landowners and iron masters was extracted.[1] Through the 20th century these towns and villages, like much of West Cumbria, suffered the effects of decline as mining slowly began to disappear and populations gradually thinned out.

In its heyday the West Cumbrian Iron Orefield drew people in from all directions – from places like Cornwall, Scotland, the Isle of Man, other parts of England and especially Ireland – during a population explosion that was so sudden, remarkable and focused upon one goal that it was compared to the California Gold Rush of the mid-19th century.

What the people who came to live in these places ended up digging for, though, was not gold but hematite. This was the mineral – as highly sought after and valuable as the Californian gold – that would be used in the iron and steel production that West Cumbria would become famous for in the 20th century. While it is the case that the smelting of iron in blast furnaces had taken place in several locations around West Cumbria from the early

18th century – in places such as Little Clifton, Maryport, Seaton and, indeed, Frizington – this was before the revolutions of the 19th century had led to technological advances in iron production that to all intents and purposes moved industry in its entirety onto a different plane.[2]

From the 19th century onwards the volume of iron produced during the process of rapid industrialisation that spread across the world was of a different order of magnitude – measured in the hundreds of thousands of tons rather than hundredweights – to what had existed before, and due to the development of new production processes, it would 'tip the balance of material civilization' as the human world was refashioned with the help of iron, steel and other metals.[3] What was taking place in West Cumbria, in other words, was part of an event – 'the event of events' in the words of historian Fernand Braudel – that might have spawned entire histories of the role of iron in the evolution of humanity, if historians had not been so bedazzled by the stories of kings and queens.[4] The deposits of hematite in West Cumbria were of the highest grade in the British Isles and fed directly into the processes developed by engineer and inventor Henry Bessemer to produce steel in West Cumbria directly from pig iron using the converter that he developed and which set the standard in steel production until the middle of the 20th century.[5]

Ordnance Survey maps from the turn of the 20th century show West Cumbria as a place pockmarked with mines and linked by a network of railway lines that had been built to move 'the vast output of iron ore, coal, limestone, and pig iron' that poured out of its countless mines, quarries, and blast furnaces.[6] In Cleator Moor – the largest town in the iron orefield – it was once said that in every garden there was an iron mine. If that sounds like an exaggeration, it was nonetheless true that buildings and churches were uprooted and relocated to allow mining to continue and that entire streets inhabited by miners and their families were dangerously undermined by the tunnelling and digging going on. It was not unusual,

⌃ Red puddles around the disused Florence Mine, at Egremont, today – now the site of Florence Arts Centre.

indeed, for houses to collapse as miners moved beneath the surface in search of the red stuff. [7]

Cleator Moor, in a nutshell, was 'built for iron, on iron, surrounded by iron and, eventually, almost destroyed by iron.'[8] As mining historian Dave Kelly has written, 'the iron deposit was so near the surface that the people living in the houses above could hear the blasting beneath them and feel the vibrations.' Yet daily life, and the work of mining, went on regardless.[9]

Beyond its peak years in the mid-to-late 19th century, hematite mining had shrunk into particular locales and continued on a much smaller scale well into the 20th century. The Cleator Moor-born artist Conrad Atkinson recalled growing up in a place that had been 'coloured by the vast hidden body of iron ore under the town', which inevitably made its way above ground and

⩔ Conrad Atkinson's miners' monument in Cleator Moor (1988), which shows a steel hand reaching out from the ground.

into the air people breathed and, indeed, the cultural atmosphere of the town.[10] There were 'paths lined with crystals from the mines, crushed red gravel on the footpaths through the town' and 'doorstops of polished hematite beside the reddened doorsteps.'[11]

The iron orefield came to be associated with the colour red because of the visible evidence of hematite so close to the surface. It is not surprising that long before it had been used in the production of iron it was, for millennia, mined for its artistic uses. Indeed, traces of hematite are found in the oldest known cave paintings, such as those discovered in the 20th century at Lascaux in France, as well as in the canvases of more modern painters. The latter produced red paint by grinding the hematite 'with mortar and pestle into a fine reddish powder', which was then 'mixed with feldspar, vegetable oils, or animal fats, to give it different shades.'[12] Atkinson, an artist in the making, was struck by the colour: he thought of the miners he grew up amongst as 'the redmen', who could be seen arriving home from work with their clothes transformed by the fine red dust 'into glittering fine silk' as if they were wearing 'postmodern haute couture', and armed with 'red offcuts of pit props' to stoke the fire at home.[13]

It was a sight that was accompanied by sounds unique to these places, not least that made by the wooden clogs that the miners wore – the only footwear that could keep feet dry and not fall apart – which were constructed of strong leather uppers and soles that had been toughened up with nailed-on metal strips that fairly clacked along pavements and even threw up sparks in cold, dark mornings.[14]

The routes around these mines, especially during the dark mornings of winter, were sometimes more easily negotiated by walking the railway lines that transported the red stuff out into the wider world. It was not unusual for men who walked the lines to develop a stride and gait that was set by stepping on the regularly spaced railway sleepers as they walked out into minefields not as easily accessed by road that had sprouted in more rural parts.[15] A place called Salter was one of the many small settlements that grew up around this area, lying close to the edge of the National Park but within walking distance of the villages of Frizington and Rowrah. Today, all that remains as evidence of its existence is an old road sign on the A5086, two-thirds of the way between Cockermouth and Egremont that reads 'Salter 1 Mile'.

In September 1953, the *Manchester Guardian* reported on the slow but gradual disappearance of what it referred to as a strange 'rural slum' in this 'Arcadian setting' that edged onto the Lake District. Salter had been a 'terrace of twenty cottages built in the late 18th century to serve an iron mine', the report stated – one of the dozens, if not hundreds that had existed here – which had ceased operating in 1912.[16] Yet, even then, 50 years later, there were still former miners, now long retired, occupying the strange, crumbling settlement that had been left to ruin by the landlords who had abandoned their property. The houses, despite looking out to 'some of the finest views of the Lakeland fells to be found anywhere in Cumbria', seemed to be so out of place and so much more characteristic of terraced rows of houses found in places like Salford than anything that one might have expected to see so close to a place that represented an escape from modern urban life.[17]

The fact that the communities in these places did not all go the way of Salter once their associated industries disappeared tells us something about how people made their homes in West Cumbria. These rows of houses, often hastily thrown up and once upon a time prone to disappear into underground mines, became places, and, collectively, the home for generations whose origins dated back perhaps no further than the inward industrial migrations of the 19th and 20th centuries.

Industrial West Cumbria left not only sites where the land had been mined for iron and coal until it had been exhausted or was no longer economically viable to bother with, but also examples – scattered all over the place, in towns and villages everywhere – of a distinctive character and atmosphere that lingers in many of its streets and houses. These can often seem like the remains of some vanished world. It wasn't long before I began to see how that past had made those streets and houses, and how they – in turn – like other examples of unique places around the world, could be understood to 'concentrate and miniaturise' their own universe.[18]

In certain places, these houses, often laid out in long unbroken rows that crowd and enclose narrow streets on both sides like some roofless tunnel into centuries past, offer up not only the most striking examples of a unique local adaptation of what we think of as the standard 19th-century terrace – a structure common across the towns and cities of industrial England – but also, more broadly, of the house as world.[19] The house as the living space in which we age and grow, in other words, becomes a 'microcosm' of 'settlement and inhabitation.'[20]

These miners' cottages can be seen standing in uniform rows near the places where hematite and other minerals were dug out of the ground. Often they are closely grouped together into several streets, and in places they can be found running in single rows – like the last remaining relics of a city that has vanished, leaving only countryside around them – alongside busy roads. The main outward and observable difference between these terraced rows of houses and their counterparts elsewhere in the country is that local practice – to help protect the houses from the elements – was to treat outside walls with render and finish off the exterior with certain details. It is common to see door- and window-frames in muted colours, which often seem to have been planned to vary the pattern with neighbouring houses. In Millom, another iron town that grew up from almost nothing at around

The sense of encountering what once must have been a world in miniature is not so much the result of the imagination as it is about the fact that places are cultural landscapes.

the same time, there is a similar attachment to the use of colour highlights on the exteriors of its terraced rows, although untreated surfaces are more common there.

In these towns and villages, the sense of encountering what once must have been a world in miniature is not so much the result of – as in the case of Norman Nicholson's representation of Millom – the imagination almost imposing spatial constraints, as it is about the objective existence of places as cultural landscapes. Where Nicholson, for instance, saw little to be imagined both 'eastward beyond the western fells' that locked Millom in and oppositely in 'the oceanic perspective westwards', the status of these places as cultural landscapes was a consequence of how they rose up to be 'organically related to their environment' in such a way that they transformed nature into place.[21]

These places and their communities were inseparably bound together in almost all aspects of life simply because they sprang into existence together, at the same time. There was no past in these places, but only the beginning and foundation that was industry, mining and the desire to remove the red stuff from the ground. That fact, on the face of it, would seem to distinguish the towns and villages

⩔ A terraced row in Cleator Moor.

of the West Cumbrian Iron Orefield, and the town of Millom, from the traditional patterns of life that the first inhabitants – industrial migrants – might have known in their homelands. It made these people, as sociologists of modernity would have it, exiles in a foreign land who embodied the idea of history as one of upheaval.[22]

In West Cumbria, the terraces that linked the homes of its miners were slightly different than those found in other counties. In fact, in many places they pre-dated terraces elsewhere that were built according to the so-called 1871 Bye-Law Housing Act, which imposed common standards across the country. Examples of the latter constructed in the late Victorian period, could be found all over the country. So, not only do the West Cumbrian variants look different on the exterior – because of the addition of colour highlights – and not only are they built often from local stone (as opposed to brick), they also differ in scale and dimension and, as such, are entirely unique to this place and possibly even unique in design and dimension to the mine proprietors who built and owned them in order to house their employees. The house, in other words, existed and reflected an entire political, social and economic world unique to its place. The same might be said of all industrial communities – from 18th-century mills to 19th- and 20th-century industrial towns and cities – that gradually become complete worlds in themselves whose centre was the house; a house whose architectural form was directly related to 'its economy, society and politics.'[23]

The miners' cottages we see around the landscape of West Cumbria now were located in close proximity to the fields where these riches were dug from the ground. In fact, you can almost guarantee that where you see a row of these houses, perhaps incongruously standing by a road that runs through the middle of open land, there was once a mine in that place that was within walking distance of the workers' homes. In a quite profound sense, everything about these homes was tied to the economic activity of their particular society and to the very land and minerals they stood on top of.

Hodbarrow Point and Lighthouse, Haverigg One of the most notable remaining structures from the industrial era to be found on the Cumbrian coast is the sea wall at this location on the Duddon Estuary near Millom. Originally running to 6870 feet in length, the wall was designed by dam engineers and erected at the turn of the 20th century in an attempt to hold back the rising waters that threatened to engulf the Hodbarrow Iron Company's workings.

Echoes

On the Cumbrian coast, Millom was the southernmost of the urban areas that comprised industrial West Cumberland. Along with other iron towns inland, like Cleator Moor, it experienced an unprecedented boom in the mid-19th century, as a result of the speed with which the iron and steel industries took off, leading to 'striking population changes' within a very short space of time.[1]

At that time, the rapid growth that had become evident probably seemed to guarantee the town's future as a 'little capital of a little mining Kingdom'.[2] Millom's hemmed-in position on the Duddon Estuary, looking out in all directions to natural boundaries and inadequate overland communications networks, saw it frequently compared to an island – not unlike its near Atlantic neighbour, the Isle of Man – when it came to the passionate local sense of loyalty that was to be found within its population.[3]

The most well-known product of Millom, besides steel, was the poet Norman Nicholson, 'the greatest Lakeland poet since Wordsworth', read an obituary in *The Guardian*.[4] But Nicholson was equally a poet of the grubby and dirty industrial Cumbria, and had been discovered by T.S. Eliot at Faber and Faber, whose own work as a poet might be described as being far from pastoral in its concerns or romantic in its leanings. Nicholson's attachment to his hometown, which some might have seen as a stubborn retreat from a broader experience of the world, seemed to be matched by the methodical labours devoted to his work. 'I like to think that when I've finished a poem you can drop it on the floor and it won't break', he once said.[5] Perhaps the same was said of the other products of Millom – the steel that flowed beneath the smoke and flames that lit up the sky around the clock.

After the ironworks that spurred on the growth of the community in those boom years closed in 1968, there was a steadfast refusal to do as many economic and industrial experts advised and simply abandon the town.[6] 'Exile', here, as elsewhere in West Cumbria during the 20th century, was frequently advocated as a solution to the troubles that certain places faced.

'Rather than moving home', *The Guardian* reported in 1976, 'Millomites travel long distances to work'; and what's more, they did so 'in part of the country where the communications are bad'.[7] So bad were the routes in and out of Millom, especially the roads, that travelling by motor vehicle was described as a 'tortuous' experience.[8] But, by the early 1970s, there was a possible solution that might have been perfect for this unique location on the fast-changing intertidal flats of the Duddon Estuary. A hovercraft-manufacturing company called Sealand – which advocated its craft as the quickest means of travel to circumvent the travel difficulties of Millom's location – was demonstrating that the tortuous route from Millom to Askam around the Duddon Estuary, which took 30 minutes by road, could be accomplished in less than two minutes for a lucky hovercraft owner.[9]

If that scenario seemed unlikely, it is only because now we can no longer see hovercraft anywhere. People under the age of 50, in fact, may never have seen or heard of these things known as hovercraft. But, not only was this a form of travel that looked to be going places in the 1970s, for a time it did indeed seem to be an idea that would lock-in with attempts to stimulate local population growth for Millom, offering a solution to the obstacles presented by its surrounding landscapes. In the wake of dreams of a coming leisure age, developers saw Millom as providing a perfect location for a new population

The tortuous route from Millom to Askam around the Duddon Estuary, which took 30 minutes by road, could be accomplished in less than two minutes for a lucky hovercraft owner.

of middle-class residents, inward migrants with a relaxed lifestyle who would be eager to transplant themselves to the new model settlement at Haverigg – modelled on a Scandinavian fishing village and built on the grounds of the old Millom ironworks.[10]

What was envisaged at the time was a community that could be large enough to support a marina, hotels and a golf course. Local residents in Millom, however, including Nicholson, had their doubts. News reports quoted him as saying that he thought that the only chance the scheme had was if the hovercraft became the adopted means of travel across and around the estuary.[11] But, by the mid-1970s, three years after the first phase of the Haverigg development was opened, the Sealand Company had gone into receivership with mounting and unpaid debts.[12]

•

Today, on parts of the land where the old ironworks once existed, the merest of traces remain of that past. In surroundings that can, at first sight, seem as green and pleasant as untouched nature, it is only the oddly contoured shape of a mound here or a raised path there as you venture forth across the land – walking on what is perhaps a former wagon track – that give a clue as to what was once located in this place.

As I traipsed over the land one summer day looking for the site of the old ironworks, it was possible to discern the sound of a loud and dull but distant mechanical pounding. It was the sound of automated clanging coming from back in the town, as if the ghosts of those Millom ironworkers who refused to die continued to invisibly operate some great steel press on the empty land I now found myself standing on.

Ravenglass Once an important base through which the Romans delivered supplies to its forts and bases in what we know today as Cumbria, Ravenglass – like much of West Cumbria – is faced by the sea to the west and by the rugged hills and valleys of the Lake District to the east. Even today, the old Roman road across Hardknott Pass, which was one of their main routes from this place, is a remote and difficult passage to negotiate without the right kind of vehicle.

Islands

There are certain places that seem to become more or less cut off from what exists around them. Even places that are not surrounded largely or entirely by water might be thought of as being rather like peninsulas or islands.

Southern California, bounded by the Pacific to its west, the Yosemite and Death Valley National Parks and the Mojave Desert to its east and Mexico to the south, has been famously described as 'an island on the land'.[1] It is a description, though, that arises as much from a sense of historical and cultural uniqueness as it does from its obvious geographical separateness. Berlin, too, provides another kind of example. It existed, for much of the 20th century, as an extreme example of how places can be defined or circumscribed by factors that have more influence on what they are, and on how people are able to live, than mere geography does. In that case, it was the existence of geopolitical forces and the armature of military might that kept the world beyond outside and shaped Berlin as a kind of island – perhaps even a number of islands, an 'archipelago' – that became as inaccessible as any island separated from land by a body of water that surrounds it on all sides.[2]

In addition to the natural and political boundaries that had set it apart as a remote or unwelcoming place, West Cumbria – as a cultural landscape – was also, like Southern California or Berlin, separated from the body of land that it formed a part of, whether this was conceived of as 'the North', as 'England' or as 'Britain'. West Cumbria, too, had something of the character of an island at certain points in its history. Economically and culturally, West Cumbria faced westwards; a recognition of the fact that trade and communications over the Irish Sea, and outward to the Atlantic, were simply more capable of being realised than were similar connections to inland population centres and markets elsewhere in England.[3] The West Cumbrians who found themselves at home in this place often arrived as migrants from other places dotted around the rim of the Irish Sea. It had existed as an area of economic and cultural exchange that went back to prehistoric times, and as such had long predated modern geographical–political notions of place identity (such as England, Britain or even the British Isles).

Modern ideas such as the nation state – linked to particular lands or territories – may be the historical novelty here, especially if we try to understand the perhaps different or unique character of places that are found on the outward-looking western coastal periphery of Britain.[4] The nation state, in fact, usually projects the sea as something that divides and separates, rather than existing itself as another 'human realm' that in important ways came first, preceding the land.[5] In this kind of view, the sea, as a great mediator of exchange and meeting, was 'the uniter of people'.[6]

West Cumbria's economic and cultural exchange across these western waters, with a number of ports acting as points of entry and departure around the Irish Sea, saw it once characterised as part of a 'British Mediterranean'.[7] It was an idea developed by a geographer named Halford Mackinder, who wrote that for the west of Britain, Ireland and the Isle of Man, the Irish Sea was more like an inland body of water that facilitated the economic and cultural exchange of these places. 'The Irish Sea is a British Mediterranean', he wrote in 1905, 'whose four sides are England, Scotland, Ireland and Wales. The mountains of all are visible from Snae Fell – the peak of

❮ **Around the edge** Over and across the Irish Sea and the Solway Firth flowed the economic and cultural connections that helped to forge modern West Cumbria. This map reveals the close proximity of the edges of Scotland, Ireland and other places on what geographer Halford Mackinder once referred to as the 'British Mediterranean'.

which rises from the midst of the Irish Sea to a height of two thousand feet, forming the summit of the Isle of Man, a fifth part of Britain, neither English, Scottish, Irish nor Welsh, but Manx'.[8]

To think in this way is to regard the sea as something that connects more than it separates, and that – of course – relates to a time in history when the sea was the principal means of communication. The world that West Cumbria would rise up in, and became part of, was akin to this British Mediterranean.

Mackinder's idea obviously had much to do with the historic economic and communication links, the ease

❯❯ ***Allonby*** Once Cumbria's best-known coastal retreat, it was later eclipsed as a seaside resort by Silloth, located a dozen or so miles further up the coast.

of access to markets afforded by the sea. It particularly reflected the truth of the fact that the most prosperous ports or nations once thrived on control of the oceans and waterways, which were used to expand economies, consolidate political power and spread cultural influences. It might be common to conjure up an image of the Mediterranean as the holiday destination of pleasure seekers that we are familiar with today, a place seemingly far from the colder northern shores of the Atlantic and the Irish Sea, but Mackinder meant to identify the role of the sea in establishing something of a common territory that gave rise to a different sense of place. In the Mediterranean itself, as Fernand Braudel showed in *The Mediterranean and the Mediterranean World in the Age of Philip II*, a common culture that had little to do with the idea of the nation state had in fact arisen over thousands of years.[9]

But, if it is historically accurate to view the Irish Sea as something akin to a mini-Mediterranean, whose existence as a distinctive cultural entity was founded on trade and commerce, then it is no less true to note that like the Mediterranean it was also subject to the vicissitudes of time and change. It was always likely to face the threat of economic decline when new forms of exchange and communication were developed, and when newer and more profitable trade routes opened up. The fact remains that the character of any place is the result of many complex factors that develop over time and history.

Long before the rise of industrial West Cumbria – which gained its riches due to its coastal location and mineral resources – the Irish Sea had 'teemed with maritime traffic through the millennia' and became a 'major factor in creating the web of cultural sharings evident around its shores'.[10]

If the only true littoral societies or communities – meaning places like the Mediterranean, where life was concentrated along the coast – are those where the interaction between the sea and the coast lands remains commonplace or a matter of daily routine, then perhaps the particular remoteness of the west coast of Cumbria, cut off to a great extent by the harsh hinterland terrain of the Lake District but opening out to the Irish Sea, did help it to function for a time like those port towns and cities on the Mediterranean, certainly during its first phase of maritime expansion. In the aftermath of its economic decline as a waterway where trade and commerce had long flourished, partly a consequence of other forms of overland communication becoming more economically viable, it did not quite manage – as the actual Mediterranean did – to reinvent itself as a holiday destination for the ages.

Nonetheless, even the most rugged and climactically unwelcoming of coastlines has its attractions. In the Romantic era of the early 18th century, when the lure of the sea saw coastal areas match mountainous landscapes as sites of sublime experience, it was because the possibility of imaginative transformation lay in the sight of storms that could be seen from the shore. The perilous and life-threatening ocean became an object of aesthetic contemplation.[11]

Perhaps the remoteness of the west coast of Cumbria, cut off by the Lake District but opening out to the Irish Sea, did help it to function as part of a 'British Mediterranean.'

In the many guides to 'watering places' (an old term for seaside resort) that were published in the 18th and 19th centuries, Allonby on the Cumbrian coast was described as one of the principal locations for sea bathing, a recommendation that was enhanced by the views it offered over the Solway Firth to the hills of Dumfries and Kircudbright.[12] But as well as the importance that was once attached to sea bathing 'as a preventive, no less than a curative process in the economy of health' – to quote one contemporary source – there was the simple pleasure to be had in being on the edge; in walking over the sands or wandering around the dunes that marked the shore.[13]

In *The Lazy Tour of Two Idle Apprentices*, a fictionalised retelling of a walking tour of Cumberland taken by Charles Dickens (Francis Goodchild in the story) and Wilkie Collins (Thomas Idle) in 1857, the resort of Allonby is spied on a map and enthusiastically identified as the perfect destination to meet their needs, 'the most delicious piece of sea-coast to be found within the limits of England, Scotland, Wales, the Isle of Man, and the Channel Islands', according to its location on the map, the two men reasoned.[14] It was bound to be possessed of 'every luxury a watering place could offer an idle man'.[15] As they approached the town by coach from Aspatria – a town whose name suggested 'the departed glories of Greece' to the excitable tourists – Idle called out to Goodchild, who had stuck his head out of the carriage window in anticipation of a view of the great sea-bathing resort, impatient to know if they had arrived yet:

> 'Do you see Allonby?'
> 'I don't see it yet,' said Francis, looking out of the window.
> 'It must be there,' said Thomas Idle.
> 'I don't see it,' returned Francis.
> 'It must be there,' repeated Thomas Idle, fretfully.
> 'Lord bless me! ... I suppose this is it!'
> 'A watering-place,' retorted Thomas Idle, with the pardonable sharpness of an invalid, 'can't be five gentlemen in straw hats [...] four ladies in hats [...] three geese in a dirty little brook before them [...] What are you talking about?'[16]

Today, Allonby is probably better known as a place along the route of the Frontiers of the Roman Empire World Heritage landscape that it now forms a part of than it is as a town on the fringe of some vanished British Mediterranean.

Workington Looking out over the Irish Sea. When Cumbria's port towns were heavily involved in shipping coal to its main markets on the other side of the Irish Sea, it was still possible to travel around the waters of what Mackinder in 1905 would refer to as Britain's 'inland sea' – this was before Ireland won its independence from the United Kingdom – when the Isle of Man steamers served Whitehaven and Silloth.

Inbetweeners

All that really remains as a reminder of the 'British Mediterranean' today are the echoes of places that once bounded it, heard in the sounds and voices that radio transmitters bring back to a place – West Cumbria – that was once at the centre of things and now exists on the periphery. 'Peripherality', in this sense, is an interesting idea, because it is not simply a geographical phenomenon given by the fact of being located on the edge or boundary of some physical area, but rather it tends to refer to the idea that places can come to hold little interest or be of no importance to most people.[1] But as such a place shifts from the centre to the edge it is possible to see it as also occupying an 'inbetween' space.

In West Cumbria, the realisation of this 'inbetweenness' hit me as I scanned the AM and FM radio frequencies while travelling by car around the coast. Once I had established a loose sense of my co-ordinates, but still in need of more information and other impressions of the place, I asked a colleague what he would do in my position. 'Well,' he said, 'listen to the local radio, and you'll soon figure out where you are.'

So, I spent much of my time on the road, looking at what was out there in front of my own eyes – on the ground, looming up in the distance – while simultaneously searching for more clues via my car's radio. This did not necessarily lead to a sense of enlightenment in terms of gleaning information about the actual place I was in, but my sense of place changed soon enough anyway. The babble of voices (and accents) began to transform my sense of the peripherality of this place – the sense of being in an 'unimportant' place without a unique or well-articulated sense of itself – into understanding it more accurately as one of those kind of transitional, 'inbetween' places. For as it turned out, West Cumbrian 'radio space' – if I can call it that – reflected its history and the limits of a cultural geography that had, in many respects, faded into the past. I found myself listening to voices that seemed to be out of place.

The voices of two Irishmen, who were located in Dublin, addressed me through RTÉ Radio Dublin, dispensing seasonal advice – turning me into one of their hypothetical 'local' listeners who were curious to know how they should utilise their gardens at this 'time of year' – and recommended that I should now be planting my 'Christmas potatoes'. 'Where?' I wondered. Was this a tip that applied anywhere within range of their broadcasts or only in Ireland? Do cultural habits, like cultural influences in the maritime age, translate to territories now divided, rather than joined together in some way, by the sea?

I suddenly had an image of some alien visitor in a similar situation being quite confused by the conflicting geographical–locational information that such radio encounters might bring to light, because the 'local' radio (that is to say, what I was able to pick up here in West Cumbria) seemed to be coming from all directions.

I soon found that I could choose between a range of voices that in all likelihood – and without need of the internet, which destroys the peculiarity of location – could only be encountered here: BBC Radio Scotland, BBC Cumbria, BBC National Radio (London), BBC Radio Ulster, Manx Radio, RTÉ Radio Dublin and Radio Clyde broadcasting from Glasgow. All this knowledge seemed to locate me anew – at the centre of a place that was somewhere between Scotland, England, Ireland and the Isle of Man, which is to say, somewhere near the geographical centre of the British Isles; not on the margin, as such, but in the middle.

If nothing else, the voices that might have temporarily given rise to a sense of personal dislocation or confusion seemed to be in tune with what I would learn about this place from historical sources, namely that in economic and cultural terms, West Cumbria was in fact once at the centre of its own small world; one that extended across the seemingly arbitrary boundaries drawn on maps and was not confined by the formations of land and water that produce in us an image of where one place ends and another begins.

The voices of two Irishmen, dispensing seasonal advice and recommending that I should now be planting my 'Christmas potatoes'. 'Where?' I wondered.

•

A tip I picked up from William Least Heat-Moon's book, *PrairyErth*, was to try and be imaginative when plotting your location on these abstractions we call maps. Following his example, I tried to centre myself.[2] I discovered that where I am is 259 miles from London (a 10–12-hour round trip by train or car), 128 miles from Glasgow (just over two hours' drive), 90 miles from Newcastle and 142 miles – as the crow flies – from Dublin, the place from where my seasonal advisors were broadcasting their gardening tips. If you look at a map of the British Isles, from its northernmost coastal edge to its most southerly tip in Cornwall, I am located very close to the mid-point of the two extremes. Similarly, tracing a straight horizontal line from where I am would establish that I am at a mid-point between Middlesbrough on the east coast of the country – where the A66 road that terminates at Workington, begins – and Belfast in Northern Ireland to the west.

I am, in other words, very close to the geographical centre of something – the political entity we know as the United Kingdom – yet, I am undeniably on the margins of things in a more profound sense; one that indicates something crucial about the character and spirit of the place as it has emerged into its present-day form.

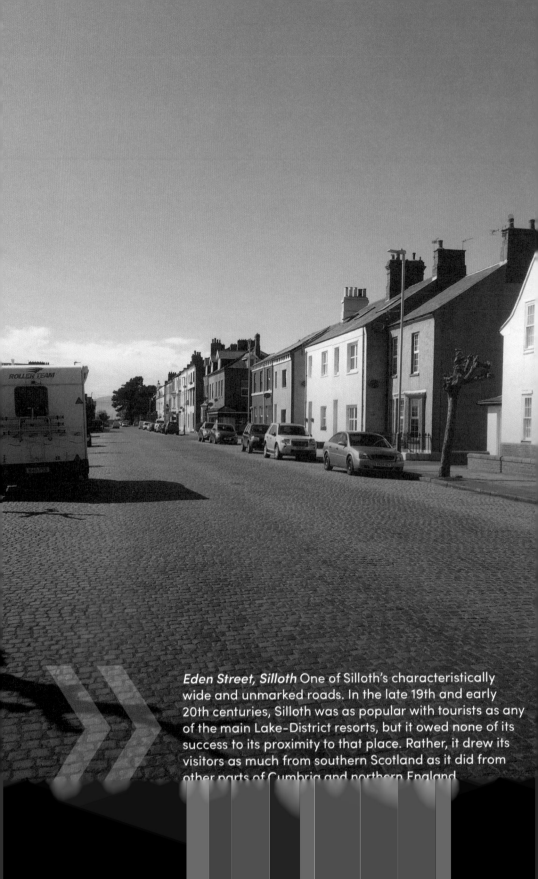

Eden Street, Silloth One of Silloth's characteristically wide and unmarked roads. In the late 19th and early 20th centuries, Silloth was as popular with tourists as any of the main Lake-District resorts, but it owed none of its success to its proximity to that place. Rather, it drew its visitors as much from southern Scotland as it did from other parts of Cumbria and northern England.

Dreamscapes

For many years I had found myself crossing between England into Scotland on the M6, over the border and back again, and I would often find myself being distracted by the road signs to places that I now know to be on the Cumbrian coast, but which for years remained obscure to me. The name of Workington, for instance, had a ring of familiarity to it – as if I knew what it looked like, when I had, in fact, never been there. Perhaps I assimilated it to somewhere else in the old mythical industrial North because of its name (if nothing else) or because of the icon of the lorry that always appeared next to the place name on the motorway exit signs. I would also notice another odd-sounding place name, Silloth, and occasionally wonder what delights it held in store.

These signs marked the exits on my route that were effectively the last chance to turn off the road before entering Scotland (or the first chance on entering England, if moving in the opposite direction). During those travels, a time before the internet and mobile phones made it easy to look up strange places and quickly satisfy any curious impulses, these were simply locations that had never registered any impression, to the best of my recollection, through the only available mass media means, things like television or newspapers. They were places, it seemed fairly clear, that would remain mysterious destinations to anyone who did not actually have a reason to visit them.

Once or twice I tried to convince myself that there was nothing else for it but to execute a dramatic late swerve – as in the movies – that would carry me off my route. Just to see what was actually out there. But then the moment would be lost as I approached the invisible border between the two nations and passed, in the blink of an eye, from one country into another. As I left the prospect of distant Silloth behind, I imagined that I wouldn't really be missing anything and that it was probably just a collection of farms set amidst a rural landscape of flat land as far as the eye could see; one where all that was to be found was endless farmland. And cows and sheep and farm vehicles. I imagined the smell of the land and the nothingness of a place that had nowhere to stop, versus the safety and dependability of the wide road ahead, with its service stations, toilets and coffee. How could I have imagined that it was actually located by the coast and was a proper seaside town, its streets lined with houses painted in ice-cream colours that looked out onto carefully spaced and manicured trees that had been pruned to look somewhat exotic. Surely there should have been signs saying 'to the seaside' or something similar?

Now my familiarity with Silloth brings to mind not only a place that is in some sense lost to time, but also one that was perhaps always out of time and place. Somewhere that is in the wrong location, in any case, here in a part of the country where there seems to be nothing around it that accounts for why it is here. This was a perception that the many barely readable, faded and rusty road signs – relics of the mid-20th century – that rose up in front of me on my way to the town fed into. But, on the other hand, these were details that made it

I imagined the smell of the land and the nothingness of a place that had nowhere to stop, versus the safety and dependability of the wide road ahead, with its service stations, toilets and coffee.

all the more fascinating. In some respects, it is a place that may essentially be no different to any of the other British seaside towns of the Victorian era – especially those located in the North – that never quite made it through the leisure transformations of the latter part of the 20th century. For the masses, whose predecessors once flocked to these seaside towns, the idea of what qualified as a suitable holiday location changed dramatically in a very short space of time. Air travel opened up the world to cheap international destinations and, not least, to the exotic: to holiday destinations where unbroken sunshine or other rather different attractions or new experiences could be guaranteed. Silloth seemed to belong to a bygone age of the British seaside. Today, outside of holiday times – when it draws in visitors from West Cumbria and from caravan parks found in this part of the county – it can seem a bit like an abandoned place; although one that is almost guaranteed to surprise anyone who visits it for the first time. Nikolaus Pevsner, once the measure of all things interesting about England's huge variety of places, praised Silloth for its 'marvellous' views across the Solway Firth to the mountainous Scottish coastline and noted that its gridded streets and terraces were 'mildly Italianate' in style.[1]

Perhaps, with its wide and expansive planted green – where people once played tennis, watched entertainers perform or were taken towards the sea in strange horse-drawn bathing machines – its Italianate streets and its manicured trees, Silloth could be best thought of as one of those rare, very early examples of what is called postmodernism; a place of contrast and contradiction that seems to have no natural roots in its terrain. As such, it is maybe not too different from other examples of transplanted Italian urban styles constructed in the same era, such as Venice in California, a 'dream city' that rose out of sandy marshland near Santa Monica, Los Angeles, but also with an eye to creating something that really belonged in another place.[2]

Silloth, the first time I visited, also reminded me of a place where I had once stopped when I was driving through New South Wales in Australia, travelling between Melbourne and Sydney. It was a Victorian town called Cessnock, which I had visited on a quiet Sunday when the streets were empty and – perhaps it was for this reason – the place also seemed to have been abandoned, its wide streets emphasising the absence of people and traffic. Silloth's own wide streets are very interesting and unusual, and one wonders why the town was laid out with so much space. It's as if some follower of Baron Haussmann, the designer of modern Paris, drew the map of Silloth's main connections, taking care to keep them straight and as wide as possible. In fact, what began with an idea to build a port for Carlisle in this location, connected by rail (the port still operates to this day, but the railway to Carlisle was closed in 1964), was overtaken by its obvious potential as one of those 'watering places' – a holiday resort of the kind that grew increasingly popular in the Victorian age.

The Carlisle and Silloth Bay Railway and Dock Company had bought up land around the railway terminus and port and provided the infrastructure of the new resort, laying out the streets, sewers and gas pipes on top of which the town would rise, seeing it as a means of generating revenue through the new railway network that was being laid down all over West Cumbria.[3] Beattie's 1842 guide to the *Ports, Harbours, Watering Places, and Coast Scenery of Great Britain*, makes no mention of Silloth, although a place named 'Silluth', probably an estate of some sort, can be seen on Christopher Saxton's 16th-century map of Cumberland in roughly the same geographical location. In retrospect, a scheme to erect such a place in this location – close to where medieval monks had settled for its remote wilderness qualities – seems like it would have been a promising initiative. With Carlisle on the main line between England and Scotland just a few miles to the

⌃ **_Silloth_** A view from Criffel Street looking out towards the green and the 19th-century pagoda shrouded by trees. Silloth was postmodern before the term had been invented. It looked then, in its 19th-century heyday – and still today – like nowhere else in Cumbria.

north, Silloth-by-the-Sea (as it was marketed) would have been an attractive destination before car and air travel became commonplace. The rail route also had the benefits of funnelling visitors to the seaside without the attractions of Lakeland getting in the way and circumventing the mountainous centre of Cumbria that essentially cut off much of the rest of the west.

When the North British Railway company took over the Carlisle and Silloth Bay Railway in 1862, it seemed to acknowledge that Silloth's most likely market would be found along the new North British Railway route from Edinburgh to Carlisle, which went through the Scottish Lowlands. This led to a boom time for Silloth that saw it match the most well-known Lake District destinations for visitor numbers, an outcome that was all the more impressive because its success had nothing to do with the proximity of Lakeland.[4]

Today, the fact that the town's main road surfaces – laid out in attractive granite setts that can easily be mistaken for cobbles – have not been altered by the addition of the kind of traffic-calming bumps found elsewhere and have been subjected to only the most minimal line markings where streets meet, adds to the perception of its being transplanted from another time and place. On the green near the roadside, a well-preserved version of the mid-20th-century black-and-white road signs that can be seen fading and rusting elsewhere around the county stands in pristine condition, the words 'Cumberland County Council' – the local authority that ceased to exist nearly half a century ago – running vertically down the striped post.

One local West Cumbrian I spoke to described Silloth to me – without so much as a reference to postmodernism – as an imaginary place. A place unlike Workington, where we stood as he told me this, a town that, by contrast, had been battered and moulded by the accelerated tempo and ceaseless grinding of the industrial age's onward progress. I could see what he meant. From the glass pagoda that is situated on a mound at the edge of the green overlooking the sea – which may have replaced an earlier pavilion that was the subject of a well-known Raymond Moore photograph – to the planted shrubbery – the trees and the rose and bee garden – Silloth seemed like a dream place. From certain vantage points – and for different reasons than those suggested by Pevsner – I sensed that it could have existed on another continent.

Certain views out across the Solway Firth struck me – no doubt helped by a bit of imaginative input – as vaguely Northern Californian in aspect or even somewhat like the landscapes of sparse Japanese ink drawings; there, in front of me, was a pine tree bent by the wind and looking as singular and out of place as an oversized potted bonsai, its outline framing the emptiness that disappeared into the distance ahead.

An 1860 article in a London periodical called *The Reasoner* first announced the existence of this

⌄ **An imagined place** The sense that Silloth is a kind of imaginary place is heightened by the planted gardens on the edge of the green and the variety of trees around its edge – both those facing the town and those facing the sea. The views here, with the help of the trees, had me thinking I could be in California, Scandinavia or Japan.

Intergalactic transport As I regularly traversed the roads in and through the Lake District, I realised that many of the caravans and motor homes on the road had strange, almost intergalactic names – or other names that promised some sublime or transformational experience.

strange place, Silloth, to inhabitants of the capital and elsewhere, following the extended holiday that had been taken in the town by the article's author, George Holyoake. Assuming the role of impartial guide to future visitors, he sketched a picture of a place that was being imagined as a resort for what he thought to be the better class of Victorian tourist; a place built to offer all the benefits of healthy retreats such as Bath or Cheltenham.[5] But during the time of his stay – some

four months in length – it was still early days for the
new resort, whose houses and pier were still 'trying to be
built'.[6] Perhaps this fact also accounted for the notable
absence of well-heeled exiles from the shires who had
abandoned Bath and Cheltenham in favour of Silloth,
which emerges from the picture Holyoake paints of
the comings and goings at his hotel. It had been taken
over by a motley assortment of patrons – 'Austrian
and French sailors, Italians from Guiseppiana, Solway
fishermen and Cumberland navvies' – who formed a
loud and drunken choir in the hotel bar. 'They all sing
together, they all want beer together, they all thump
the table together,' he reported. The problem was that
they didn't really seem to be able to comprehend each
other, a fact that was obscured from the men by the
flow of alcohol that had so relaxed them in each other's
company. And so, as the bar was closed by its impassive
landlord, Holyoake recounted, disappointment quickly
followed, and the assortment of voices and accents
tumbled out onto the street to do the only thing that
was left with the night, which was to fight out their
differences.[7]

Silloth almost found a twin town in Seascale,
where the idea for a similar railway resort further
south on the Cumbrian coast had been developed but
went uncompleted. That place, since transformed by
Cumbria's nuclear industries whose scientists moved en
masse to the town in the 1950s, had once been known as
a small, remote, sea-bathing resort.[8] Like Silloth, it was
intended to be laid out on a central grid that opened out
onto 'boulevards, promenades, and crescents to equal
anything offered by Bournemouth or Eastbourne', yet
unlike Silloth, it never made the transition from the
imaginary into actuality.[9] But if Silloth was, and still
is, a kind of imaginary place, what of those other parts
of Cumbria where the tourists flocked, then and now?
Is not 'Lakeland' – or *Wordsworthshire*, as it was once
referred to in recognition of the crucial role that one

man's imagination played in making it the place it is today – an imaginary place, too?[10]

On the road during my early travels to the Cumbrian coast, I was always reminded of how hopeless it was to try to reconcile the kind of overly confident time and distance calculations we all make when we are travelling – *60 miles, well that will be about one hour, won't it?* – with the reality. The road had many narrow and impassable stretches that lasted for miles and were also used by a wide variety of slow movers: farm vehicles, cyclists, those run-of-the-mill slow drivers who spend as much time looking out at the landscape while doing 40mph as focusing on the road ahead and – of course – the ubiquitous caravans and motor homes, heading for one of their various natural habitats. The feeling of travelling in the direction of somewhere that was set apart from the conventional and everyday was heightened by the sight of these vehicles – great numbers of them – which are probably to be found heading for remote places everywhere. *Why not buy a car AND a hotel, too?!* the adverts for 'mobile homing' and DIY holidays in 'the middle of nowhere' used to run.

The small and compact mobile home, it seems, always needs the contrast of something that is correspondingly vast – the sea, giant mountain ranges, desert sands and so on.

The people who inhabited these vehicles, whether static or moving, had often been portrayed as a bit strange ('people who enthusiastically participate in such recondite pastimes as reversing competitions', as Jonathan Meades once wrote) or the cause of great eyesores on the landscape ('there were many tin caravans on the coast', Paul Theroux wrote on a 1982 tour around Britain, 'that would make a useful blaze').[11] But I soon came to the realisation that the caravaners and mobile homers were really just dreamers of an open space in which a shrunken form of domesticity – tiny bathrooms and cookers, small plates and teacups – might make contact with the infinite. The small and compact mobile home, it seems, always needs the contrast of something that is correspondingly vast – the sea, giant mountain ranges, desert sands and so on.

Many of these vehicles, as far as I could tell, seemed to have been named in honour of transcendent journeys. Perhaps, like their destinations – places that come to life through a thousand imaginary projections – they were intended to effect a psychological transformation, marking the fact that the escape from the chronic drudge of the workaday world began as soon as you set foot in your vehicle and did not have to wait until you made it to the destination.

One oddly branded vehicle was named, rather magnificently, I thought, the *Gypsy Rapture* – a name that obviously had me thinking of transportation to a post-apocalyptic heaven – while other models suggested that whatever the route taken to any particular Holidayland, the mode of travel promised no less than change or renewal – a spiritual or exotic encounter perhaps – thus, the *Swift Spirit*, the *Kon-Tiki* and the *Swift Royale*. Royale spelt with an 'e' is not even a word in the *Oxford English Dictionary*, yet instinctively you know on seeing or hearing it that it is meant to suggest luxury – superior in class and ability to satisfy desire, a kind of *royal-plus*. Another class of these cruising tin boxes – mostly caravans towed by cars – seemed to signify a hankering for celestial travel: I spotted vehicles with names such *Quasar*, *Cosmos* and *Solaris*, as well as countless others I could not make a note of because I was too busy trying to overtake them.

•

Perhaps the names reflect a simple truth that anyone who takes ownership of one of these wagons has been seduced by ideas of a boundless existence, fallen hostage to imaginative projections or understands already that where they are going is not real in some way. And what is so wrong with that?

Whitehaven past A view of a street in the old town. In the 17th century, Whitehaven was the first post-medieval town to be built in England, and today it remains one of the most complete Georgian towns in the country. The other main port towns on the coast – Maryport and Workington – also contain distinctive Georgian cores, around which Victorian and later 20th-century streets and buildings rose up.

Pasts

In the last quarter of the 20th century, a mania for preservation gripped the post-industrial regions of the world. It ushered in a new recognition of the value of relics from that past, including those districts of towns and cities – and their streets and buildings – where some functional purpose had suddenly disappeared. The attention paid to the past through the new heritage and preservation movements was not evenly applied and depended in large part on the efforts of local activists who could see the value of places that were in danger of being caught up in that other 20th-century whirlwind – modern town planning – that saw so much of the suddenly old and shabby industrial world swept away to be replaced by something more modern.

Parts of West Cumbria had been successfully industrialised quite early; the historic core of Whitehaven, for instance, faced onto and served a port that was still visibly a place of industrial activity into the latter part of the 20th century. What today can be seen as its past, in other words, was still then the place of its living and working present. The places of the industrial world had, in so many ways, always existed on the edge of the future, and the idea of preservation could not take hold until certain ways of life, and certain kinds of work, had ceased to be viable. The evidence of the 17th- and 18th-century origins of West Cumbria as a place once modern in aspect and built character can still be found in its several Georgian town cores. Parts of Maryport, Workington and

⋀ ***Whitehaven present*** New buildings on the fringe of Whitehaven maintain some consistency with the character of the Georgian town core.

Whitehaven remain recognisably the same as they have been for hundreds of years and will continue to do so as more efforts are made to preserve their historic features.

In Maryport, the town grid, inspired by Whitehaven and built in 1748–49, remains intact and seems unusual in this part of the world: a bold statement of 17th-century modern intentions. It leads onto a quayside that – as Nikolaus Pevsner noted in the 1960s – is, by contrast, 'all humble and villagey'.[1] Whitehaven, likewise, is frequently mentioned as one of the few English towns that has more or less preserved a historic Georgian core (despite some questionable 20th-century additions that have baffled architectural historians). In his 1986 book, *The Architecture of Northern England*, John Martin Robinson noted that the town had only latterly started to preserve the best of its historical core, noting that 'part of the pleasure for the visitor to Whitehaven consists of improving the place in the mind's eye, as with some care it could still be a very handsome town'.[2]

The peripheral location of these towns may account in part for the fact that what was historically characteristic about them wasn't swept aside in a wholesale manner, as happened in so many parts of the industrial world in the 20th century, to make way for newly imagined urban spaces that often erased historical traces altogether.[3] That fact makes some of the towns on the West Cumbrian coast as unique and interesting – if not as well preserved in all cases – as many of the places that were celebrated in the recent Informed Conservation series of English Heritage books: a series of studies, in truth, of the relationship between the built environment of particular places and their working and industrial cultures.[4] The most obvious changes that have been made to Maryport and Whitehaven are around the harbours – both of which have added new houses – and marinas, which provide berths for many small sailing boats. The newer additions foster more of a sense of leisure, although small numbers of working vessels can still be seen.

In terms of understanding these places within the more recent general trend towards 'place-making', it took a long time for industrial societies to discover the prevailing historical sensibility – preservation – that guides the work of the various heritage industries. It was a development that reflected the fact that 'the past, the various pasts, are culturally original' and might have some interest to people now and in the future.[5] Many places were too caught up in the relentless flow of historical time to notice that the remnants of vanished ways of life might be of some value to posterity.[6] In some places, such as West Cumbria, where no replacement industries seemed to be appearing in an era when entire local economies were dominated by single industries, economic depression loomed for many long and hard decades, and relics from the recent past – the leftovers of its redundant industries – were mostly regarded as eyesores or dangerous structures that had to be removed.

The change that divides present-day attitudes from the period when post-industrialisation was really taking hold – the early part of the second half of the 20th century – is evident in the difference between Pevsner's original guides to the architectural heritage of England, dating from the 1960s, and its revised successor volumes, which were published early in the 21st century: the original guides showed little or no interest in the country's industrial heritage, but the later, updated versions, in sharp contrast, not only make a point of looking at 'industrial remains', but can also be withering in their criticism of local authorities that had swept aside industrial sites of some historical importance.

One such example in Maryport is the now vanished 18th-century blast furnace that in its day worked with the latest technology and had been, in terms of capacity, the biggest and most advanced in Britain. Matthew Hyde notes that the furnace had 'stood complete until 1963, when the site was cleared in an act of extraordinary vandalism'. [7] There are, though, remains of several coke ovens that fed the vanished furnace. These have been legally protected since the turn of this century under legislation that was originally designed to protect ancient monuments and archaeological sites. That, in itself, tells a story about how time and history play out in unexpected ways.

When representatives of local authorities with responsibility for the towns and cities of Britain's north-west met at a 'Regional Coastal Conference' in the mid-1960s there was no consideration given to the role that such 'heritage' might play in reviving the fortunes of places on the Cumbrian coast. [8] The movements to preserve the built cultural heritage of working places had not yet emerged in any coherent or uniform way, and as a consequence the post-industrial leisure and tourist potential of towns like Maryport and Whitehaven – along with other Cumbrian coastal towns – was viewed almost entirely in terms of the opportunities the coast offered to absorb excess day visitors from the tourist hotspots in the central Lake District, which is to say, to offer coastal picnic areas and places to fly kites, as opposed to anything culturally specific to the heritage of West Cumbria as a unique place in itself.[9]

But historic places are now seen, in much broader terms, as having provided the setting or context that would have conditioned the outlook and life rhythms of their

⩔ *Georgian echoes* The practice of using one colour for the walls and another for the door and window surrounds was probably not a feature of the original Georgian town.

inhabitants, whose specific cultural habits or environmental sensibility – their intangible culture – is often as interesting as what remains of the built environment.[10]

Sometime towards the end of the 20th century, scholars began to talk about places in new ways, suggesting that they could be seen as almost text-like in their qualities, displaying on their surfaces – their streets and buildings – marks and symbols of time and history that made them 'unconscious' repositories of a kind of cultural memory. This urban unconscious was to be found in the traces that remained unchanged throughout time and in relics dug out from places that had been hidden or subdued in the process of change. The search for evidence of the past of a place is something that contemporary culture has become more attuned to, and is one important way of recognising the power of this image of an 'urban palimpsest'. The idea that places preserve traces in such a manner refers back to the ancient parchment-like documents – palimpsests – that were used, erased and written over repeatedly, but which allowed the trace of older texts or messages to show through. Within the context of understanding how places negotiated the line between the past and the present, that idea became a means of coming to terms with how places unfolded in time.[11]

The peripheral location of these towns may account in part for the fact that what was historically characteristic about them wasn't swept aside in a wholesale manner.

In Whitehaven, while each new era left its mark on the town as it spread out and grew beyond the historic core and up and over the steep hills that surround the town – the landscape that made it an obvious harbour location – it is in the centre that the 'present past' can really be seen in a small, contained space. This, perhaps, has much to do with the fact that in its original design and layout – dating from the 1640s and employing the orthogonal grid that is 'ubiquitous' in the history of urban settlements – it was really intended, like most grid systems in history, to be expanded outwards from its core.[12] It just so happens that

≫ *Whitehaven past* Detail from an 18th-century engraving. Pevsner's guide observes that Whitehaven – with its gridded layout – gives a flavour of what the North American ports may have been like in the 17th and 18th centuries.

in this case, the outward expansion came much later and, as such, betrays the traces of different eras, which had their own forms and functions.

•

The flat land that Georgian Whitehaven was built on was ideal for the kind of gridded design that had begun to be laid out in port cities elsewhere in Europe (particularly in the Netherlands) in the 1600s. As the first modern town to be built in England, after hundreds of years during which little had been added to the 'Roman towns, Saxon towns and some 400 or 500 post-Conquest towns of the 12th and early 13th centuries', its prospects for greater urban expansion were also ultimately limited by the peculiarities of its location.

Distant from the main urban centres of England at the dawn of the railway age, and with ports unable to expand to match the capacity of the larger cities on the west coast of the country, West Cumbria became isolated out on its edge.[13]

On the Edge The Sellafield site, Britain's most extensive nuclear landscape, lodged between the land and the sea, and the present and the future. This was first the site of Calder Hall (1956) and Windscale (1951) – the former producing electricity, the latter plutonium – now either largely dismantled or beyond use. The site was renamed Sellafield in 1981, although very old maps reveal that the area was historically known as Sellafield.

Futures

From the 18th century onwards, the Lake District became known as one of the great locations to experience the much sought-after extremes of the 'mountain sublime'.[1] But even for those who preferred something more relaxed than climbing great heights in contemplation of the terrifying beauty of nature, it offered an escape from the noise, dirt and stress of the everyday world. The landscapes of West Cumbria, by contrast, presented something else entirely. Rather than the open space, clean air and elevated viewpoints afforded by the Lake District, West Cumbria was a place darkened by smoke, soot, grime and pollution. It contained countless mines – probably numbering in the hundreds – ensuring that here, as elsewhere in industrialised parts of the country, a whole underground world was opened to its people, whose occupations took them into darkened and enclosed spaces.

The gradual disappearance of the dirt and grime of the coal-powered world from the skies and the built environment of West Cumbria – leaving behind scattered relics where mineworks once existed – was eased by the development of new power sources and new technologies. The nuclear industries that were developed here and elsewhere in the world during the 20th century to produce electricity and atomic weapons were less visible in terms of their operations and effects. Instead, what people saw and heard were images and ideas about the shape of a coming 'Atom Age' of human civilisation. This was the time when the first waves of what newspapers referred to as the 'Atom Men' moved into West Cumbria. They were 'quiet men with craggy brows and thoughtful eyes, with portfolios full of notes and heads full of world-shattering ideas' who had unveiled the future to come, said *Illustrated* magazine in 1955.[2]

Here, in the place that was built over and excavated the energy source of the first industrial revolution – coal – the new future would be built on cheap, abundant, atomic energy, as seen in the illustrations of smiling housewives preparing meals on electric hobs that were to be found in the sparkling kitchens of tomorrow. The future then, in such visions, was not the long-distant, incomprehensible and far-off future, but rather the tomorrow that was just around the corner.

West Cumbria's nuclear industries, which have effectively replaced the older industries that grew up here specifically because of its location, also made their homes here because the geography was right. Sellafield demanded a location that was remote and close to 'large sources of cooling water'.[3] West Cumbria had the Irish Sea but there was also, a few miles inland from Sellafield, Wast Water, as well as another body of water suitable for supplying drinking water to an expanded population, which was made available by the damming of Ennerdale Water in the late 1940s. This was just one of many contested technological incursions into the Lake District that were intended to improve life and work in West Cumbria.[4] And, in fact, West Cumbria's life-lines and tendrils extended into that other Cumbria: from its power lines and water supply to its new roads through the Lake District. Opposition to the use of Ennerdale Water to supply the industries and populations of West Cumbria came not only from those whose concern was the damage that would be done to a landscape of outstanding natural beauty, but also from other unlikely sources: one developer objected on the grounds that he believed his own plan – to build an opera house, holiday homes and leisure facilities on the land around Ennerdale Water – would be a more fitting use for the spectacular natural setting of the location.[5]

If Sellafield had been a 19th-century industrial plant responsible for the same number of livelihoods (directly and indirectly) as it is today, it would have been surrounded by a small city: one that would be large enough to accommodate not only its workers – who would have lived without the kind of geographical mobility we enjoy today – but also their families, dependent industries, ancillary services, outlets for leisure and entertainment and everything else that urban life has typically offered. What West Cumbria is, as a consequence, is a kind of dispersed and micro urban region made up of a number of smaller urban places – its main towns – which exist together as West Cumbria yet at the same time hold on to their own distinctive character and identity. The West Cumbria that extends beyond Sellafield and Drigg – once described as the UK's 'graveyard of nuclear waste' – today seems to unwind the clock.[6] The traveller passing through these places might feel as if they are going backwards in time into a place that looks and feels much like mid-20th-century Britain.

But there on the coast at Sellafield, somewhere within buildings that have risen up around activities that remain mysterious to most of us on the outside, the work will proceed silently and out of sight even beyond 2020 when the Magnox Reprocessing Plant is due to close. The only visible and tangible evidence of it as a place to anyone who has no business being there is its presence as you pass through on the coastal train or as you drive close by. If you are lucky to be travelling south at the right time of day in the autumn or winter months before dusk becomes night, it is possible to be caught by surprise by the remarkable sight of endless streaming traffic, pouring in an unbroken single line out of tree-lined farmland when the Sellafield shifts change over. A procession of paired headlights can be seen snaking slowly in the darkness all the way from the plant itself to Whitehaven and then beyond until they have dispersed and their drivers have been delivered into distant and unseen homes around West Cumbria and beyond.

What is also there, beyond this sight, is another more permanent one on the edge of green fields where the land meets coast and sky; you can see it, perhaps, not simply as something occupying the skyline but as something that takes on strange forms depending on the viewing angle or time of day. A 'Martian castle' as Paul Theroux once wrote.[7] Or perhaps, as darkness falls it shapes up as a glowing presence that – in the words of local poet John Gibbens – takes on the appearance of 'a city-sized battleship' that has pitched up at the edge of the land.[8]

At Sellafield, since the end of the Second World War, the idea of the future has taken on another dimension. The legacy waste from plutonium and nuclear energy production accumulated at the site projects West Cumbria into a non-human kind of temporality; one more akin to the geological scale. Nuclear waste – unlike any other kind of waste – is unique in that it is of a kind that 'resists its own containment' and, as such, presents peculiar challenges.[9]

Here, in the place that was built over and excavated the energy source of the first industrial revolution – coal – the new future would be built on cheap, abundant, atomic energy.

The human scale of time, which provides the context of our day-to-day experience (even when it touches upon our futures), is relatively modest in scope and, indeed, is often marked by the repetition of 'seasonal' events – birthdays, anniversaries, school terms, sporting seasons, political cycles – that give the years ahead 'a rhythm' that directs our sense of what lies in front of us.[10] But even more than this, is the issue of future predictability within the human scale. Governments, for instance, come and go in a handful of years, and economists and other forecasters unerringly fail to predict what will happen with any certainty as little as a decade ahead in time. Within that kind of context of experience of the future, the other future of the nuclear heartland has to exist and to move on a different, entirely separate, temporal track.[11] It is worth remembering that the written traces of human civilisations – which is to say, our knowledge of human history – only go back a few thousand years. But here, the issues being faced will have implications for this place and beyond for a period that extends a lot further in the opposite direction.

This, in other words, is a place whose future may possibly extend far beyond the (relatively speaking) brief interludes that mark our own time on this planet, never mind the usually shorter periods of time during which we may find ourselves attached to one specific place or another. Indeed, if we think in terms of our own lives, it can be hard to grasp the idea of a future beyond that of our children or grandchildren. The notion of something existing for a 'long time' seems to be constrained not only by our own limited knowledge and experience, but probably also by an awareness of how much has changed in the world around us in our own lifetimes. The 20th century – the century when nuclear industries were developed – was a period marked by remorseless change; an unpredictable time when what happened at various junctures – the arrivals of supersonic jets, space travel and artificial intelligence and the computer revolution in everyday life, amongst other developments – could probably not have been predicted half a century before.

The other Cumbria of the Lake District is a place that exists as a singular kind of timescape whose dimensions extend beyond the scope of lived human historical experience, going further back in the other direction into what many perceive to be a kind of immemorial pre-history when those mountain ranges were thrown up. West Cumbria, by contrast, has a different kind of relationship to time. West Cumbria has a different kind of relationship to time, which ensures that the two Cumbrias offer contrasting versions of the sublime: the natural versus the technological.

Seascale Close to the location of Britain's most extensive nuclear landscape, as well as the sites of historical and contemporary military weapons testing. This is a place that is emblematic of West Cumbria's unique 'edgeness' – by the sea and always on the edge of the future.

Temporalities

West Cumbria, like many places, is a strange place – a place that does not reveal itself so easily. But it is perhaps unique in being at once ancient, medieval, modern and futuristic. In some places you will see evidence of prehistoric settlements. By the River Ehen at Beckermet, a hamlet close to Sellafield on the Cumbrian coast, evidence indicates that in around 4000 BC primitive humans had already begun to modify the environment, burning areas of forest that were thought to have existed around their camps.[1] This trend towards modifying the human landscape is carried on in various ways through all human history. Grey Croft Stone Circle, an arrangement of Bronze Age standing stones, sits in a field opposite the site of Sellafield; the ancient staring at the modern in a location that is also close to a proposed – and futuristically imagined – nuclear power station at Moorside.

It is impossible to make sense of a place without realising how it has been shaped by its history, that much seems true – but what of a place that seems to point to an open-ended future? It is common to take for the 'historical' that which is merely old or has its origin in some past that we have now become distanced from. It is equally common to see the same idea of history in the things around us that have clung on to their place in the world – ruins, long-standing built structures, settlements, landscapes – as time continues to move forward. But history also refers to a process of change that is *forward-directed* and consciously pressed into the service of human needs and their various schemes and desires. This all can exist alongside other places and ways of life that *don't* change or that seem to have existed since some immemorial past. Such places may seem old, places like Cumbria's Lake District, but they might not be truly historical in that sense of holding a position in the present that is open to a drastically different future.

It is the experience of change that alters our perspective on the world around us, and our relationship with the past today, in the here and now, which is – of course – also always slipping into the future. Time is a very complex phenomenon that we make sense of by aligning ourselves with certain rhythms or cycles, much like people did long before they had clocks and calendars and utopian dreams of some better future. Places and people exist in time and carry time forward, making human landscapes into what might be called *timescapes*.

To move through the landscape, towns and other places of Cumbria is to be confronted with a place that is made up of different kinds of temporal experience, but also different temporal scales. In some places, signs of change are very clear to see and – in terms of built structures or industry – often point towards the future; in other places, there seems to have been an absence of significant observable change, and one feels the presence or echo of the past. West Cumbria offers unique and distinctive examples of how time and history shape a place and leave their stamp on it, whether that is seen in cultural, economic or environmental terms. Yet, the sense of temporal or historical 'layering' does not, for the most part, seem forced or manufactured (unlike some places in the country that seem much more affected by the contemporary heritage consciousness that developed in the second half of the 20th century).

⌃ ***On the edge of the Western Lakes*** A view of the Wasdale
Screes from the edge of Wast Water, the deepest lake in
England. The loose lower surface of the rising form might
be mistaken – certainly when their lofty pointed peaks
have disappeared behind mist – for some kind of industrial
slag heap.

The pattern of habitation on the low-lying rural
parts of the county to the west, for example – including
the settlements that grew from hamlets and villages into
larger towns on the coast – was established around a
thousand years ago, after the Norman occupation. The
Cumbrian landscape that is known by everyone as being
characterised by lakes and mountains exists, in one
sense, in geological time. In terms of its broad features
and topography, it predates human settlement patterns
and subsequent changes to the land that have resulted
from the spread and growth of human populations.
But the Cumbria of romantic imagination, born of

⌄ **On the edge of the future** Around eight miles from the
scene at Wast Water and close to the coastal location of
Sellafield is the site of the proposed Moorside nuclear
power station. This design proposal for the administrative
building at Moorside Power Station was released in 2016 as
part of NuGen's public consultation and illustrates one vision
of the future for West Cumbria.

the 18th century, does not represent a static world; it is a managed world and one that has been shaped by how people have adapted to and made use of the land that is part of a larger place that has been remade by human interactions over several thousands of years. The evidence of temporal scale – reaching from prehistoric to futuristic – is maybe not that unique to this part of Britain, and in fact almost any place one looks at will soon betray more historical depths and layers as it is examined more closely, but it is perhaps a more distinctive feature in West Cumbria because of the nature of the places that represent the extremes of the temporal–historical scale.

At some point during my travels into Cumbria, moving from east to west and back again, the contrast between the two distinctive parts of the county struck me as existing at two opposite ends of a temporal spectrum that was quite uncertain in its extent – whether one looked to what seemed to be the apparently unchanging pre-human landscapes (the Lake District) or to the always changing parts and – even more so – the futurist Cumbria of nuclear technologies (West Cumbria).

It was a journey that felt like a movement from the eternal and immutable to a place that seemed to have been in continual flux; a place that exhibited much more of the fabric and messiness of a human history that churned through time and plundered the very land it settled itself on without much concern for how it might preserve its own past. West Cumbria, it seems, had always been a dynamic, expanding place. It was a more obviously humanly shaped world that, by contrast with the other Cumbria, pointed itself towards the future. And, through time and change, and as economic currents ebbed and flowed since the 16th century, it had become more historically layered as it tried to shape itself to fit a future that was usually precarious.

•

What lies within the bounds of the Lake District, of course, is no less a landscape that is today – and has been – shaped through all kinds of human use and intervention. It also has its own history of smaller-scale industrial and manufacturing industries that pre-date modern industry, but it is nonetheless preserved in certain respects to reflect an image of a particular kind of place; an image that dates from the 18th century and from the Romantic discovery of wild, sublime, spiritual nature. By the very nature of its topography and landscape character – and, of course, the fact that it has remained sparsely populated – it appears at first sight to be one of those unchanging places, akin to the imagined landscapes of the numerous Arcadias that have been represented in the history of art. Come to the place that inspired Wordsworth, the guidebooks will say, and this, of course – the possibility of seeing in the landscape what he and others saw – remains its great attraction.

But from a place where one might encounter something that is greater than human – something spiritual or sublime, which exists as a kind of shock absorber for the modern urban dweller on retreat – the journey through Cumbria leads ineluctably towards a place imbued with human history. This is a place where the ghosts and echoes of 19th- and 20th-century industries find a home on ground that is contrastingly flat for the most part; a landscape whose existence had so long depended on its proximity to the sea. A land that has also been, throughout its history, variously Viking, Roman and fought over by Scotland before it was finally English; a place that was Cumberland before it was Cumbria and, more recently in its history, a destination for generations of modern industrial migrants.

> From a place where one might encounter something that is greater than human – something spiritual or sublime, the journey through Cumbria leads ineluctably towards a place imbued with human history.

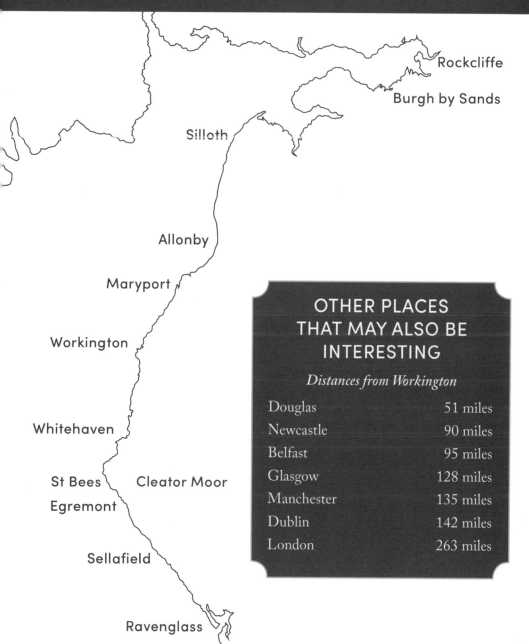

MAP OF PLACES ON THE EDGE

Rockcliffe

Burgh by Sands

Silloth

Allonby

Maryport

Workington

Whitehaven

St Bees   Cleator Moor

Egremont

Sellafield

Ravenglass

Millom

OTHER PLACES THAT MAY ALSO BE INTERESTING

Distances from Workington

Douglas	51 miles
Newcastle	90 miles
Belfast	95 miles
Glasgow	128 miles
Manchester	135 miles
Dublin	142 miles
London	263 miles

End notes

Locations

1. John Martin Robinson, *The Architecture of Northern England* (London, 1996), p. 39.
2. See Arto Haapala, 'On the Aesthetics of the Everyday' in *The Aesthetics of Everyday Life*, Andrew Light and Jonathan M. Smith (eds) (New York, 2005), pp. 42–43.
3. Robinson, *The Architecture of Northern England*, p. 65.
4. Haapala, 'On the Aesthetics of the Everyday' pp. 48.
5. See Christian Norberg-Schulz, *Genius-Loci: Towards a Phenomenology of Architecture* (New York, 1980), p. 11.
6. See J. Nicholas Entrikin, *The Betweenness of Place: Towards a Geography of Modernity* (Basingstoke, 1991), pp. 6–26, 132–34.
7. Yi-Fu Tuan, *Topophilia: A Study of Environmental Perception, Attitudes and Values* (Englewood Cliffs, NJ, 1974), p. 113.

Frontiers

1. *Encyclopedia Britannica*, 8th Edition, Vol. 7 (Edinburgh, 1842), p. 578.
2. Christopher Hill, *The World Turned Inside Out: Radical Ideas During the English Revolution* (London, 1991), p. 73.
3. See Kristian S. Gleditsch, *All International Politics is Local* (Ann Arbor, MI, 2002).
4. Quote from Peter Davidson, *The Idea of North* (London, 2005), p. 224; Alex Woolf, *From Pictland to Alba: Scotland, 789–1070* (Edinburgh, 2007) notes that 'Cumbria comprised most or part of Lanarkshire, Dunbartonshire, Renfrewshire, Stirlingshire, Peeblesshire, West and Mid-Lothian, eastern Dumfriesshire and Cumberland' p. 155. See also, William Rollinson, *A History of Cumberland and Westmorland* (London and Chichester, 1978), pp. 45–48.
5. Marc Morris, *A Great and Terrible King: Edward I and the Forging of Britain* (London, 2008), p. 362.
6. See David Brett, *A Book Around the Irish Sea: History Without Nations* (Dublin, 2006), p. 76, which describes it as a 'square mile' that contains 'notable militaria from AD 150 to 1300 to 1940'.
7. Peter C. Newman, *The Empire of the Bay: The Company of Adventurers that Seized a Continent* (London, 1998), p. 383.
8. Evan Thomas, *John Paul Jones: Sailor, Hero, Father of the American Navy* (New York, 2010), p. 11.

Prospects

1. On the length of the Cumbrian coast, 75 miles is the length of historic Cumberland (as was) given by William Whellan, *The History and Topography of the Counties of Cumberland and Westmorland* (London, 1860), p. 24; 100 miles was the figure given after the creation of the new county of Cumbria, in Roger Smithells, 'Costa Cumbria' *The Guardian*, 17 May, 1975, p. 16.

2. Tim Hamlett, 'Tail End Charleys' *The Guardian*, 19 July 1976, p. 7.

3. See details in J. D. Marshall and John K. Walton, *The Lake Counties from 1830 to the Mid-Twentieth Century* (Manchester, 1981), pp. 46–47, 86.

4. David Gissen, 'Urban Intrusions: A Reflection on Subnature' in *Urban Constellations*, Matthew Gandy (ed.) (Berlin, 2011), p. 37.

5. R. G. Collingwood, 'Roman Signal Stations on and off Hadrian's Wall' *Transactions of the Cumberland and Westmorland Antiquarian and Archaeological Society*, Series 2, Volume 29 (1929), p. 161.

6. *Ibid.*

7. William Whellan, *The History and Topography of the Counties of Cumberland and Westmorland* (London, 1860), p. 464.

8. Andrew Gibson, '"At the Dying Atlantic's Edge": Norman Nicholson and the Cumbrian Coast' in *Coastal Works: Cultures of the Atlantic Edge*, Nicholas Allen, Nick Groom and Jos Smith (eds) (Oxford, 2017), p. 83.

9. 'Industrial Cumberland: Two Ruined Towns' *Manchester Guardian*, 12 June 1934, p. 11.

10. *Ibid.*

Images

1. Quotation from Ian Jeffrey, 'Photography at Weeping Ash: Ray Moore Talking' *Creative Camera*, March/April (1981). Peter Turner, *History of Photography* (London, 1987), p. 148.

2. John Roberts, *Photography and its Violations* (New York, 2014), p. 139.

3. On Moore capturing 'cultural wholeness' see Elizabeth Edwards, 'Beyond the Boundary' in *Rethinking Visual Anthropology*, Marcus Banks and Howard Morphy (eds) (New Haven and London, 1997), p. 59.

4. Melvyn Bragg, 'Preface' to *Every So Often: Photographs by*

Raymond Moore, Neil Hanson (ed.) (Newcastle upon Tyne, 1983).

5. See Mark Howarth-Booth, 'Current Comment: Joseph Koudelka' in *Creative Camera: Thirty Years of Writing*, David Brittain (ed.) (Manchester, 1999), p. 15.

6. Jeffrey, 'Photography at Weeping Ash' p. 148.

7. The quotation is from Jeffrey, 'Photography at Weeping Ash' p. 148. Allusion to 'grey' draws on Jonathan Williams, 'Raymond Moore (1920–1987)' in *A Palpable Elysium: Portraits of Genius and Solitude* (Boston, MA, 2002), p. 158.

8. Vilém Flusser, *Towards a Philosophy of Photography* (London, 2000), p. 9.

9. See David E. Nye, *American Technological Sublime* (Cambridge, MA, 1999), p. 109.

10. Fernand Braudel, *The Structures of Everyday Life (Civilization and Capitalism, 15th–18th Century, Vol. 1)*, trans. Siân Reynolds (London, 1981), pp. 373, 375.

11. See, for example, Daniel Pick, 'Stories of the Eye,' in *Rewriting the Self: Histories from the Renaissance to the Present*, Roy Porter (ed.) (London, 1997), p. 190.

12. Siegfried Zielinski, *Deep Time of the Media: Toward an Archaeology of Hearing and Seeing by Technical Means* (Cambridge, MA, 2006), p. 31.

13. Lance Keimig, *Night Photography* (London and New York, 2012), pp. 3–30.

14. Joachim Schlör, *Nights in the Big City: Paris, Berlin, London, 1840–1930* (London, 1998), p. 275.

15. On the way postcards turned photographs into writing surfaces, see François Brunet, *Photography and Literature* (London, 2009), p. 93.

Westwards

1. Matthew Hyde and Nikolaus Pevsner, *Cumbria: Cumberland, Westmorland and Furness (The Buildings of England)* (New Haven and London, 2014), p. 526.

2. See Caron Egerton Newman, 'Mapping the Late Medieval and Post Medieval Landscape of Cumbria' PhD Thesis, Newcastle University (2014), Vol. 1, p. 89.

3. The description is in J. E. Marr, *Cumberland* (London, 1910), p. 5.

4. See David Cooper, 'The Post-Industrial Picturesque? Placing and Promoting Marginalised Millom' in *The Making of a Cultural Landscape: The English Lake District as Tourist Destination, 1750–210*, John K. Walton and Jason

Wood (eds) (London and New York, 2016), p. 241.

5. Norman Nicholson, 'Maiden's Song' in *Collected Poems* (London, 1994), p. 35.
6. *Ibid.*
7. On the first point, Gibson, 'At the Dying Atlantic's Edge' p. 80, who observes that Nicholson's poetry is a 'poetry of the Atlantic edge'.
8. Norman Nicholson, 'The Pot Geranium' in *Collected Poems*, p. 180.
9. Norman Nicholson, *Sea to the West* (London, 1981), p. 30.
10. *Ibid.*
11. Peter Davidson, *The Last of the Light: About Twilight* (London, 2015), p. 9.
12. Fiona Stafford, 'The Roar of the Solway' in *Coastal Works: Culture of the Atlantic Edge*, Nicholas Allen, Nick Groom and Jos Smith (eds) (Oxford, 2017), pp. 41–60.

Shorelines

1. See John Mack, *The Sea: A Cultural History* (London, 2011), p. 85.
2. John Stagg, *Minstrel of the North, or Cumbrian Legends* (London, 1810), p. 114.
3. Robinson, T*he Architecture of Northern England*, p. 39.
4. Philip Sheldrake, *Spaces for the Sacred* (Baltimore, MD, 2001), p. 91.
5. *Ibid.*, p. 91.
6. Nikolaus Pevsner, *Cumberland and Westmorland (The Buildings of England)* (New Haven and London, 2002), p. 170.
7. National Parks Commission, *The Coasts of North-West England* (London, 1968), p. 46.

Redlands

1. See Dave Kelly, *The Red Hills: Iron Mines of West Cumberland* (Ulverston, 1994), p. 16.
2. H. A. Fletcher, 'The Archaeology of the West Cumbria Iron Trade' in *Transactions of the Cumberland and Westmorland Antiquarian and Archaeological Society*, 1, 5 (1881), p. 5.
3. See summary and further references in Fernand Braudel, *The Structures of Everyday Life (Civilization and Capitalism, 15th–18th Century, Vol. 1)*, trans. Siân Reynolds (London, 1981), p. 374.
4. *Ibid.*, p. 373.

5. Robert William Rennison, *Civil Engineering Heritage: Northern England* (London, 1996), p. 115.

6. William McGowan Gradon, *The Track of the Ironmasters: A History of the Cleator and Workington Junction Railway* (Grange-over-Sands, 2004), p. 7.

7. See 'Mining under Cleator Moor' *Manchester Guardian*, 30 July, 1913, p. 10.

8. Kelly, *The Red Hills*, p. 21.

9. *Ibid.*

10. Conrad Atkinson, 'Common Sights' in *Conrad Atkinson Landescapes* (Claverack, NY, 2006), p. 22.

11. Atkinson, 'Common Sights' p. 22.

12. Michel Pastoreau, *Red: The History of a Colour* (Princeton, NJ, 2017), p. 18.

13. Atkinson, 'Common Sights' p. 22.

14. As recalled in British Library Sound Archive, 'National Life Story Collection: Lives in Steel – Joseph Edgar'. See: https://sounds.bl.uk/Oral-history/Industry-water-steel-and-energy/021M-C0532X0039XX-0001V0# (accessed 25/10/18).

15. *Ibid.*

16. 'A Village Called Salter: The Case of a Rural Slum,' *Manchester Guardian*, 4 September, 1953, p. 12.

17. *Ibid.*

18. Quote from Peter J. Wilson, *The Domestication of the Human Species* (New Haven, CT, 1991), p. 68.

19. On the terrace as the predominant form of working-class housing in England, see M. J. Daunton, *Housing the Workers, 1850–1914: A Comparative Perspective* (London and New York, 2015), p. 7.

20. Joseph A. Amato, *Surfaces: A History* (Berkeley, CA, 2013), p. 68.

21. On Norman Nicholson, quotes from Andrew Gibson, '"At the Dying Atlantic's Edge": Norman Nicholson and the Cumbrian Coast' in *Coastal Works: Cultures of the Atlantic Edge*, Nicholas Allen, Nick Groom and Jos Smith (eds) (Oxford, 2017), p. 84. 'Organically related to their environment' – the quotation is from Christian Norburg-Schulz, *Genius-Loci: Towards a Phenomenology of Architecture* (London, 1980), p. 10.

22. See, e.g., Peter Wagner, *Theorizing Modernity: Inescapability and Attainability in Social Theory* (London, 2001), pp. 103–106.

23. Daunton, *Housing the Workers*, 1850–1914, p. 14.

Echoes

1. See T. H. Bainbridge, 'Cumberland Population Movements, 1871–81' *The Geographical Journal*, Vol. 108, No. 1/3 (July–Sept. 1946), pp. 80–84.
2. Quoted in Alan Harris, 'Millom: A Victorian New Town' in *Transactions of the Cumberland and Westmorland Antiquarian and Archaeological Society*, Series 2, Volume 66 (1966), p. 449.
3. See Tim Hamlett, 'Tail End Charleys' *The Guardian*, 19 July 1976, p. 7.
4. See 'Norman Nicholson, Lakeland Poet' *The Guardian*, 1 June 1987, p. 2.
5. *Ibid.*
6. John Ardill, 'Let Millom Die' *The Guardian*, 12 Oct 1968, p. 9.
7. Tim Hamlett, 'Tail End Charleys' *The Guardian*, 19 July 1976, p. 7.
8. National Parks Commission, *The Coasts of North-West England*, p. 10.
9. 'Hovercraft took just 100 seconds to cross estuary from Millom to Askam' *North-West Evening Mail*, 13 December 2013.
10. 'Millom Prepares for Middle-class Invasion' *The Guardian*, 30 May 1975, p. 7.
11. *Ibid.*
12. Tim Hamlett, 'Tail End Charleys' *The Guardian*, 19 July 1976, p. 7.

Islands

1. Carey McWilliams, *Southern California: An Island on the Land* (Salt Lake City, 1973).
2. Theo Deutinger, 'Berliphery' in *Archaeology of the Periphery* (Moscow, 2013), p. 132.
3. See Louis M. Cullen, *Anglo-Irish Trade, 1660–1800* (Manchester, 1968), pp. 82–83.
4. Some recent books include: John Kerrigan, *Archipelagic English: Literature, History and Politics, 1603–1707* (Oxford, 2008); John Brannigan, *Archipelagic Modernism: Literature in the Irish and British Isles* (Edinburgh, 2014).
5. Brett, *A Book Around the Irish Sea*, p. 12.
6. *Ibid.*
7. H. J. Mackinder, *Britain and the British Isles* (London, 1902), p. 20.
8. *Ibid.*, pp. 20–21.

9. Fernand Braudel, *The Mediterranean and the Mediterranean World in the Age of Philip II*, Vol. 1 (Berkeley, CA, 1995).

10. Barry Cunliffe, *Facing the Ocean: The Atlantic and its People* (Oxford, 2001), pp. 34–35.

11. See Alain Corbin, *The Lure of the Sea: The Discovery of the Seaside in the Western World, 1750–1840* (Berkeley, CA, 1994), pp. 124–127.

12. George Bradshaw, *Bradshaw's Handbook: 1861 Railway Handbook of Great Britain and Ireland* (London, 2014), p. 63.

13. William Finden, *The Ports, Harbours, Watering-places, and Coast Scenery of Great Britain* (London, 1842), p. 62.

14. Charles Dickens and Wilkie Collins, *The Lazy Tour of Two Idle Apprentices* (London, 1890), pp. 223–24.

15. *Ibid.*, pp. 223–24.

16. *Ibid.*, p. 224.

Inbetweeners

1. See 'Introduction: The Paradox of Peripherality' in Frances Brown and Derek Hall, *Tourism in Peripheral Areas: Case Studies* (Clevedon, 2000).

2. William Least Heat-Moon, *PrairyErth: (A Deep Map)* (Boston, 1991).

Dreamscapes

1. Pevsner, *Cumberland and Westmorland*, p. 189.

2. Reyner Banham, *Los Angeles: The Architecture of Four Ecologies* (London, 1971), p. 158.

3. See W. R. Smith, 'Silloth: A Product of Yesterday' *Industrial Archaeology Review*, Vol. 3 (1978), pp. 75–85.

4. Marshall and Walton, *The Lake Counties from 1830 to the Mid-Twentieth Century*, pp. 198, 199.

5. 'Secular Diversions in Silloth' *The Reasoner*, 15 January 1860, p. 17.

6. *Ibid.*

7. *Ibid.* 'Guiseppiana', used in this quotation as a place name, does not seem to have any apparent reference to a real place today. As such, Holyoake's reference is somewhat unclear, but it seems he was using an informal and possibly archaic term to describe a part of Italy.

8. Rollinson, *A History of Cumberland and Westmorland*, p. 113.

9. *Ibid.*, p. 113. See also Marshall and Walton, *The Lake Counties from 1830 to the Mid-Twentieth Century*, pp. 196–99.

10. Keith Hanley, 'The Imaginative Visitor: Wordsworth and the Romantic Construction of Literary Tourism in

the Lake District' in *The Making of a Cultural Landscape*, John K. Walton and Jason Woods (eds) (Aldershot, 2013), pp. 113–32.

11. Jonathan Meades, 'Foreword' to Gareth Iwan Jones, *Caravan: A Great British Love Story* (London, 2015), n.p.; Paul Theroux, *The Kingdom by the Sea: A Journey Around the Coast of Great Britain* (London, 1983), p. 182.

Pasts

1. Pevsner, *Cumberland and Westmorland*, pp. 159–60.
2. Robinson, *The Architecture of Northern England*, p. 65.
3. M. Christine Boyer, *The City of Collective Memory* (Cambridge, MA), p. 19.
4. Some of the titles of which include: *The Birmingham Jewellery Quarter* (2000), *Manchester's Northern Quarter* (2008), *Bridport and West Bay: The Buildings of the Flax and Hemp Industry* (2006), *The Hat Industry of Luton and its Buildings* (2013).
5. Fredric Jameson, *Archaeologies of the Future* (London, 2005), p. 284.
6. See John Scanlan, *Memory: Encounters with the Strange and the Familiar* (London: 2013), pp. 40–48.
7. See 'Coke ovens at the southern end of Furnace Road' (List Entry Number:1019211), Historic England: https://historicengland.org.uk/listing/the-list/list-entry/1019211 (accessed 29/09/18).
8. The word 'heritage' appears once in the 103-page document. See National Parks Commission, *The Coasts of North-West England*, pp. 17, 44–45.
9. *Ibid*, p. 45.
10. Jameson, *Archaeologies of the Future*, p. 284.
11. Andreas Huyssen, *Present Pasts: Urban Palimpsests and the Politics of Memory* (Stanford, CA, 2003), p. 7.
12. See Spiro Kostoff, *The City Shaped: Urban Patterns and Meaning Through History* (London: Thames & Hudson, 1991), p. 116.
13. *Ibid.*, p. 31.

Futures

14. Robert Macfarlane, *Mountains of the Mind: A History of Fascination* (London, 2003), p. 18
15. 'This is the Atom Age' *Illustrated*, September 10, 1955, p. 11.
16. Sefryn Penrose, *Images of Change: An Archaeology of England's Contemporary Landscape* (Swindon, 2007), p. 125.

17. See 'Whitehaven's Case for the Ennerdale Scheme' *Manchester Guardian*, 2 Oct 1946, p. 3.

18. *Ibid.*

19. Penrose, *Images of Change*, p. 125.

20. Paul Theroux, *The Kingdom by the Sea: A Journey Around the Coast of Great Britain* (London, 1983), p. 217.

21. John Gibbens, 'A Wild Inhabitation' in *Collected Poems* (London, 2000), p. 24.

22. Peter C. van Wyck, *Signs of Danger: Waste, Trauma and Nuclear Threat* (Minneapolis, MN, 2005), p. 5.

23. Marc Augé, *The Future* (London and New York, 2014), p. 9.

24. Barbara Adam, *Timescapes of Modernity* (London and New York, 1988), pp. 8–10.

Temporalities

1. On Prehistoric Cumbria, see Rollinson, *A History of Cumberland and Westmorland*, p. 12.

About the author

John Scanlan is an academic who works in cultural history and aesthetics. He is the author of many books and articles, including *On Garbage* (2005), a book-length essay on 'waste', and more recently *Memory: Encounters with the Strange and the Familiar* (2013) and *Easy Riders, Rolling Stones* (2015). He is also the founder and Series Editor of Reaktion Books' 'Reverb' series, which publishes studies by leading scholars on the relationship between music and place.

Educated at the University of Glasgow, he has worked as an academic for over two decades, during which time he has held positions at the Universities of Bristol, Glasgow, St Andrews and Manchester Metropolitan University.

He is a research fellow with In Certain Places at the University of Central Lancashire.

About this book

This book is the outcome of research undertaken in collaboration with In Certain Places at the University of Central Lancashire. It is the first of a series of publications on 'place' that will explore the distinctive cultural characteristics of West Cumbria as part of a project that runs from 2017 to 2020. The research has been funded by the Samuel Lindow Foundation, an independent educational charity located in West Cumbria.

In Certain Places is an artistic research project, led by Professor Charles Quick and research fellow Elaine Speight, with the support of research associate Rachel Bartholomew in the School of Art, Design and Fashion at the University of Central Lancashire.

Established in 2003, In Certain Places seeks to generate new and creative ways of inhabiting and informing the future of places through an ongoing programme of artistic interventions. Interdisciplinary in nature, and spanning a range of art forms, its work includes temporary public art works and architectural commissions, artist residency and research projects, and public talks, discussions and events. Collectively these activities generate new understandings of the urban environment, enable new ideas to be tested in public spaces and instigate ongoing collaborations between artists, academics, urban planners, activists, public institutions, businesses and other individuals and communities in the places it works and beyond.

Photo acknowledgements

The author and publishers wish to express their thanks to the following sources for illustrative material and/or permission to reproduce it:

Photos by the author: cover, pp. 6, 9, 12, 14, 20, 25, 47, 48, 52, 58, 62, 66, 70, 75, 77, 78, 82, 84, 87, 96, 99; Dreamstime: pp. 14 (King Edward 1st Monument © Stocksolutions), 34 (Braystones Beach Sunset © Terrence Armstrong), 37 (Coast © Peter Cripps), 44 (Mineral: Hematite © Jarous), 54 (Lighthouse on the Shoreline at Millom, Cumbria © Kevin Eaves), 46 (Coastline, West Cumbria, UK © Kevin Eaves), 90 (Sellafield © Neil Kendall); Google Maps: pp. 40, 61; Library of Congress, Washington, DC (John Paul Jones Statue, 1910): p. 19; Raymond Moore, *Every So Often* (Newcastle upon Tyne, 1983): p. 26; NuGeneration Limited: p. 100; Christopher Saxton's *16th Century Maps: The Counties of England and Wales* (Chatsworth, 1992), p. 4.

Acknowledgements

The author would like to thank Michael Heaslip, Rick Wylie and Irene Rogan for guided tours of places in West Cumbria; Charles Quick for sharing his insights and methods, and for a number of productive walking-and-talking trips; Petra Tjitske Kalshoven for some critical observations; Celia Mackenzie, Miranda Kirschel, Adrian Lochhead, Heather Burroughs, Urara Hiroeh, John Sidney, Kristian Skrede Gleditsch and Steve Pickering for kindly reading and responding to drafts of the text after I had foisted it upon them; my UCLan research colleagues in West Cumbria, Suzanne Wilson, Ursula Pool and Stephen Haraldsen, who shared – whether or not they were aware of doing so – observations, information and insider knowledge about the place that helped to feed my curiosity. I would also like to thank Amy Johnson, whose local knowledge allowed me to tweak a small but significant detail in the book just before going to print.

Finally, I would like to express my gratitude to Bonnie Craig, for taking on the task of designing and copy-editing the book, and thus helping to make it the fine object you now hold in your hands.